# The
# Fast Days
# Cookbook

LAURA HERRING

# The Fast Days Cookbook

## Delicious & Filling Low-Calorie Recipes for the 5:2 Diet

hardie grant books

# Contents

# Welcome to the 5:2

# Note on Recipes

150
KCAL — Recipe calorie counts indicated are *per serving* or item.

≤150
KCAL — Where there are recipe variations, the headline calorie count is given as less than or equal to the highest calorie count for a recipe.

10 — Where there are multiple variations of recipes, individual calorie counts are indicated separately.

+10 — Additional calories for optional extras are also indicated separately, with a plus sign.

# Introduction

The 5:2, or the 'fast day' diet, is a diet for food lovers: no food groups are cruelly banished and most of the time you can continue to enjoy eating all your usual favourite treats – so you really *can* have that slice of cake on the Friday afternoon bakery run or indulge in that cheese toastie on Saturday morning. And you don't have to look like a total bore at that work do or friend's birthday, passing on all those delicious-looking canapés and champagne. It's a diet that works with your lifestyle, not a diet that ends up controlling you.

**So how does it work?** Five days out of seven you eat like a normal person, and on the other two days you reduce your calorie intake to one-quarter of what you usually need. That's it. Without having to count calories every day, it's much less monotonous and restrictive than other diets, meaning you're more likely to stick with it and see results. And as it's just two days a week, even if you're struggling a bit mid-afternoon while you get used to those fasting days (although you'll quickly find they're not at all hard to manage), you can remind yourself that 'tomorrow I can eat what I want!'. How's that for a diet?

Of course, you can't literally eat *whatever you want* on those other five days – you still have to stay within what is recommended for you, taking into account your gender, age, activity levels and current weight – but it makes those dieting days so much easier, knowing you'll be back to normal the following day.

**How many calories do I need?** As it's all a little dependent on your lifestyle, there's a bit of wriggle room, but the average suggested amounts are 500 calories per day for women, and 600 calories per day for men on fast days. This is based on average daily amounts of 2,000 calories per day for women, and 2,500 for men. But these are generalised averages;

if you know you are taller, shorter, more or less active, or lighter or heavier than the average, then it's probably a good idea to get a more exact calorie amount using one of the many online calculators.

**What can I eat?** You can, in theory, eat anything you like on your calorie-restricted days, but it makes sense to opt for food items that contain fewer calories so you can make them go further, rather than blowing them all on a breakfast burrito by 9 a.m. However, so many calorie-restricted diets recommend plans where you're eating lots of low-calorie ingredients that just fill you up or tide you over – and before you know it you're eating mainly rice cakes. Now, I've nothing against a rice cake (I eat a lot of them, usually smothered in peanut butter), but if you're eating fewer calories, surely you should make each one *really count*?! Not waste them on flavourless ingredients that purely act as fuel? And that's where the recipes in this book come in.

**The recipes in this book.** If you usually enjoy cooking and eating good food and maybe even have an (un)healthy Instagram obsession with other people's dinners, then why should that stop on the days when you eat less? The recipes in this book are calorie-controlled versions of the foods we like to eat every day. Each calorie is working HARD and earning its place on our plates. Recipes make generous use of those low-calorie flavour powerhouses, like herbs and spices, and they balance textures and flavours to really deliver meals that will satisfy you so you won't even feel like you're on a diet – well, that's the idea anyway! They are also designed so you can eat them with your family or partner, or even when you have people round – you can easily add a few extras like rice and breads or a few sides to bulk them out for the others. The recipes also aim to give you a good dose of vitamins and minerals – often noticeably lacking from low-cal food substitutes. You still need to be eating the good stuff! Just a bit less of it.

**When do I do the fast days?** Most people start off with two days per week, and choose to complete those days not immediately following one another. You *can* do them together,

but when you're starting, it can take a bit of getting used to, so it's easier to space them out. Monday and Thursday are good ones for me: far enough apart that I don't feel hard done by – there's a 'normal' day just around the corner – and not impacting on the weekend or that tricky mid-week hump day. But part of the beauty of this diet is that you can move them around to suit what is in your diary – if you've a big night out or lunch with your family on a day you had planned to fast on, then just swap them over.

Some people choose to do three fast days per week, while others, once they've seen the weight loss they need, reduce to just one. Studies have shown that even one day of fasting can help maintain weight, as well as reaping all the other endless health benefits (more of which on the following pages).

I'd also recommend that you don't fill your fast days with back-to-back meetings or intense exercise classes. Go easy on yourself. And make sure you get enough sleep: one of the main causes of overeating is tiredness – and dehydration – so stock up on that $H_2O$. Once you're an old hand at the 5:2, you can definitely reintroduce exercise into your fast days – but keep it fairly gentle.

**Won't I be HANGRY?** Yes, to be brutally honest on your first couple of fast days you probably will be a little bit at times. If you're the kind of person who thinks about food *a lot*, and you are usually planning your next meal while you're still eating your first one, then reducing your calories like this is going to take a bit of getting used to. But I PROMISE YOU, you will soon find them so much easier, and then you'll feel proud of yourself, and it will just be part of normal life. I promise. And when you see all that lovely weight loss as well as the other health bonuses, you'll maybe start to even enjoy them. Well, at least not mind them! Especially as it means you can eat all those other delicious foods on the other days totally guilt free.

**How should I spread out the calories?** If you *always* eat breakfast, then you should also do so on your fast days. At least while you get used to it. The 5:2 is the kind of diet that can fit in with your normal routines very well. The recipes in this book have ideas for breakfast, lunch and dinner, as well as snacks to keep you going. But it's very personal how you choose to split up your calories throughout the day. Most people tend to find that if you can hang on until lunch, then it makes it a little bit easier as you can then have more calories to divide across the rest of the day. Also, saving up at least some of your calories for the evening means you can enjoy a proper evening meal and won't find yourself hungrily staring at other people's dinner while you munch on a celery stalk. But see what works for you. There are plenty of recipes in this book at calories ranging from 50–350, so you can mix and match (see the menu plans on page 150–152 too). And, of course, although the recipes are in sections by meal type, you don't have to follow them rigidly! Who doesn't love breakfast for dinner?

**So, apart from weight loss, what else is good about this diet?** The answer is 'they're still finding out!' But many doctors and biologists sing the praises of what is officially called 'intermittent fasting'. One major advantage you'll notice almost immediately is that it reintroduces you to how your body is really feeling. So often we eat out of habit or boredom or because it's 'time for lunch'. But when you're on a fast day, you'll actually recognise when you feel hungry in a way you probably haven't in a while. Although it's a bit annoying and frustrating feeling hungry at first, soon you'll realise that it's just a natural feeling and doesn't have to be answered *that minute*. It's just your body reminding you to eat again at some point. You'll also find that hunger comes and goes so that's why if you have a glass of water or a cup of herbal tea, you may find that it goes away again. But what's most amazing is that this new awareness about your body spreads into your non-fast days too. Without even realising it, you'll probably find you don't want to eat that whole pizza you were dreaming of on your fast day because you're just not that hungry. You'll find you just don't need it. It brings yourself more in tune with your body in a very healthy way.

Less immediately obvious benefits, as you can't actively *see* them, are thought to include a reduced risk of developing certain cancers and dementia, and improved insulin sensitivity. This last one is a biggy. When we eat, our bodies produce insulin; if we are constantly eating throughout the day, we are constantly producing insulin as our body helps us balance those spiking blood-sugar levels. If we eat less often, then we have fewer insulin spikes, and our bodies become more efficient and sensitive to it – and it's less stressful for our bodies. An added benefit is that when we are not producing insulin, we are able to burn more fat. Double win. A decreased insulin sensitivity has also been linked to all kinds of hormonal issues (as well as an increased risk of developing diabetes), so getting it under control has more far-reaching benefits than we may realise.

It also appears that our bodies use that fasting time wisely. The science behind this involves a trip back to see how we used to live. I'm a big believer that our bodies and how they function still closely resemble those of our ancient ancestors who spent their days running around hunting and living in caves. In fact, even a hundred years ago our 'modern' diets would be mostly unrecognisable. I think we all know by now that we should be eating more natural ingredients in their natural form, but even eating three meals a day with a mid-afternoon snack is not how our cave parents lived. They would often go for a lot longer than we usually do without eating while the next hunt arrived in town. And it seems that our bodies are well designed for dealing with those longer gaps between meals. Studies have even shown that in those brief 'fasting' periods our bodies do a quick inventory to make sure we are in good condition to deal with a longer fasting period should that happen – damaged cells are healed and generally our bodies are checked over, leaving them in a good state to deal with fasting.

There are endless studies showing positive results from the 5:2. To me, it makes sense as a way to eat because it mirrors how we used to eat: we can enjoy our twenty-first-century diets five days a week, while paying respect to our ancestors on the other two days.

**Can I do it long-term?** Yes! This diet is more of a change of attitude than a diet in the conventional sense. And, once you've got the hang of your fast days, you'll find you have no problems fitting them into your lifestyle.

THE FAST DAYS COOKBOOK

# 10 Rules of 5:2

The 5:2 is very simple and that's a big part of its popularity and success, but a few rules – or *signposts* – will help make everything a bit more enjoyable and easy to slot seamlessly into your lifestyle.

**1**   **Get organised.** If you remember only one rule, then this should be it. No one wants to be caught out come 1.15 p.m. after a dull finance meeting that overran, hungry at the sandwich shop. In one moment of weakness, you can derail your whole day. So PLAN AHEAD. Know exactly what you will be eating and when, so you don't find yourself running through various food options and getting even hungrier while you work out how many calories your favourite sushi box has. And if you even suspect you might get the afternoon munchies, then pack a snack. You don't have to eat it, but it's there just in case. A majority of the recipes in this book can be packed up and taken with you in your bag so you only need to unpack your picnic come lunchtime or snack bag with the (herbal) tea run.

**2**   **Make sure you have the right tools for the task.** Getting organised also means investing in all the right kit – you don't need a lot, but make sure you have a good set of scales to weigh things out so you get exactly the right number of calories, and also decent lunchboxes and soup flasks so you can take your meals with you. I like those glass boxes you can get now; they're heavier, but they just seem better for you and your food than warm plastic.

**/3/**    **Don't eat depressing food.** As I've already mentioned, just because you are eating fewer calories, does not mean you should be wasting those calories on flavourless, soulless foods. Make each calorie work hard to earn its place. If you enjoy eating, then you should also enjoy eating on your fast days. Don't suddenly stop eating real foods. Just learn how to get more bang for your calorie buck by balancing flavour and textures, and introducing a range of ingredients to keep mealtimes interesting. It will make you feel like you've eaten something really substantial.

**/4/**    **Figure out what works for you.** And by this I mean how you spread your calories throughout the day and what days are best for fasting. Give a few options a try: maybe you can get by on only a small lunch and save most of your calories for dinner time, or maybe you really need a solid meal in the middle of the day, but can have a snack in the evening. Maybe Tuesday is a busy day when you're on your feet until you collapse on the sofa at 8 p.m.; if so, it's probably not the best day to reduce what you eat. Make the diet fit into your lifestyle, not the other way round. And remember, lots of the recipes in this book are designed to work with the other people in your life too, so there's no need to eat alone – just add some rice or pasta, or a baked potato or some crusty bread, and they will get all the calories they need, so you can all enjoy the same meal at the same time. It makes the whole diet day much more pleasant – as well as more realistic.

**/5/**    **Don't blow all the good work on non-fast days.** One of the huge and lasting benefits of all those fast days is that you will become much more aware of when you are *actually* hungry even on non-fast days, instead of when you just fancy a snack or think it might be a good idea to have just a little bite to eat while you wait for dinner to cook. Having said that, one of the very best things about the 5:2 is that you know the next day you can eat what you want. Except that, if what you want is a family-sized pizza with extra cheese, then you won't be seeing the weight loss you hoped for. Just be sensible – you know what you should be eating.

**6 / Avoid the oil.** As soon as you start getting out the pans, you'll probably also be thinking about using oils or other fats to cook with. When you're making meals on the 5:2, piling up fresh ingredients is your best bet. But when you do cook – because sometimes you really need a hot meal – then steaming is the most obvious choice. (You can use a steamer, or make little foil parcels with a splash of some kind of liquid in the oven.) You'll also find some of the recipes in this book 'fry' things in water. Obviously this is not the most delicious way of cooking your onions, but if those 'fried' onions are part of a stew or larger dish that is packed with other delicious flavours, then you really won't notice – well, certainly not enough to make it worth blowing a whopping 120 calories per tablespoon of olive oil. Occasionally it makes sense to commit a few kitchen crimes.

**7 / Learn what ingredients give you more bang for your culinary buck.** As you increase your intake of fresh vegetables, think about reducing your refined carbs, which as we all know cause blood-sugar spikes and ultimately leave you feeling hungry and tired again sooner. Opt for slow-release carbs, wholegrains, and lean proteins. It's also important to think about how to balance what's on your plate. So, as well as the above, aim for an interesting mix of textures – something smooth with something crunchy; a combination of flavours to keep your taste buds interested – and think about using lots of low-cal fresh herbs instead of regular salad leaves, adding a bit of chopped chilli or a grating of fresh ginger or lime zest to give you a flavour boost. Also, treat yourself with something that seems just too luxurious for a diet day. Prawns (shrimp) feature a lot in this book for that reason (just make sure they are responsibly sourced). They feel like a special treat, but are surprisingly low in calories while being a good protein source, and you don't need many to feel like you've enjoyed something more suited to a feast day. A grating of Parmesan cheese is another surprisingly good diet day companion as it has such a strong flavour you only need the tiniest amount, but it feels so un-diety. And obviously keep an eye out for hidden calories, like milk in tea – opt for black tea and coffee or even better, herbal or fresh mint.

**/ 8 /** **Stock up your store cupboard.** As we know, being unprepared is not a 5:2 dieter's friend. So that you are never caught hungry, keep some essentials on standby – tinned tomatoes can be quickly made into a Basic Tomato Sauce (see opposite page) to serve with a little fresh fish, or to which you can add some spices and an egg to turn it into Shakshuka (see page 106), or leave out the egg and have Bloody Mary Soup (see page 58), or you can spread it on flatbreads to make pizzas (see page 117) or use it in the Cannellini Bean & Chorizo Stew (see page 109). A few tins of chickpeas (garbanzo beans), a packet of quinoa, some prawns (shrimp) in the freezer, fresh herbs – coriander (cilantro), mint, basil – a box of eggs (a loyal 5:2 ally!), lemons and limes, some fresh ginger, harissa paste, chillies and lots of dried spices – cumin, coriander, turmeric and ginger – are my go-tos. Think strong flavours with few calories that you can add to most dishes to quickly boost their flavour profile.

**/ 9 /** **Get to know your calories.** This one is a bit boring, but once you have a rough idea of what's what, then you will be well on your way to constructing your own diet day meals and will know in a flash what you should avoid and what you can add more of. Read the backs of packets and use online resources so you start to understand where those calories add up. Know what a teaspoon and tablespoon of those ingredients you use a lot of contain so you don't have to keep looking them up.

**/ 10 /** **Plan long term.** Batch cook, freeze and make ahead. These are all helpful when you're dieting so you don't find yourself wandering the supermarket aisles on the way home from work eyeing up the 2-4-1 deals on ice cream. Plenty of the recipes in this book are designed to make in larger batches to freeze for a later date, or to make ahead and finish off just before eating. Make sure you have all the right storage equipment and portion everything out carefully – and label and date them. There's nothing worse than defrosting a mystery block of something to discover that it's cherry pie filling and not a spicy tomato sauce.

# Basic Tomato Sauce

SERVES 4

The recipes in this book are all simple and designed to remove the stress from fast days, but sometimes you need a quick fix. Below is a reliable recipe for a basic tomato sauce that I *always* have in portions in the freezer. You can add spices and it's a Middle Eastern dream, or herbs and you have a taste of the Mediterranean. It's really the most reliable sauce in the world and I couldn't be without it on fast days – make a huge batch and freeze it in portions.

2 onions, chopped

1 garlic clove, chopped

2 × 400 g (14 oz) tins tomatoes

salt and freshly ground black pepper

1 teaspoon vinegar

'Fry' the onions and garlic in a little water in a frying pan, for about 5 minutes, until soft. They won't brown but will become translucent.

Add the tinned tomatoes, season with salt and pepper, and simmer for about 30 minutes until thickened. Stir in the vinegar and simmer for a couple more minutes. Leave to cool then portion up, label and freeze.

# Simple Dressings

**EACH MAKES**
enough for
2 salads

Salads are obviously a good thing on a fast day – piles of fresh and crunchy ingredients to fill you up and make you feel great. But when it comes to dressings, we can undo all that good work in one generous drizzle. However, no one likes a naked salad. Sometimes a squeeze of lime or lemon juice and some salt and pepper is all you need, but occasionally you need a bit more than that. Here are some dressings that provide a lot of flavour from relatively few calories.

## Chilli, Coriander & Lime

Deseed and very finely chop ½ red or green chilli. Mix together with 2 tablespoons chopped fresh coriander (cilantro) leaves, the juice of 1 lime and a little water. This dressing won't keep as long as some of the others here, as the herbs will lose their freshness so it's best to make it when you need it.

## Orange & Ginger

In a small bowl, whisk together 50 ml (2 fl oz/¼ cup) freshly squeezed orange juice, 1 teaspoon freshly grated ginger and 1 teaspoon chilli flakes (leave out the chilli if you don't fancy such a fiery dressing). Season with salt and pepper. Keep in the fridge and use within a couple of days.

## Reduced Balsamic Dressing

Gently warm 3 tablespoons balsamic vinegar and 2 teaspoons honey in a small pan over a low heat until thickened – about 10 minutes. It should coat the back of the spoon but still be liquid. Cool before serving.

## Tahini, Lemon & Garlic

In a small bowl, whisk together 1 tablespoon tahini with the juice of 1 lemon and 1 crushed garlic clove (optional). Loosen with a little water to your desired consistency. This one will keep in the fridge for a few days.

Orange & Ginger

Reduced Balsamic
Dressing

Tahini, Lemon
& Garlic

Chilli, Coriander
& Lime

# Breakfast

The most important meal of the day! Although some fasters actually find that skipping breakfast stops them feeling hungry for longer, for others, something to eat before you set out on that commute is simply non-negotiable. This chapter contains a wide range of calorie options depending on how you want to weight your calories throughout the day. From a 45-calorie 'muffin' (sorry, no chocolate chips in this one) to a more substantial 265-calorie quinoa porridge (see pages 30 and 50), you can mix and match depending on what works for you. And, of course, you don't have to only have these for breakfast – if you end up eating a larger-than-planned lunch then most of these will also make a great light dinner or snack.

# Breakfast 'Muffins'

**MAKES 6
'muffins'**

1 slice of
unsmoked bacon,
chopped

3 small eggs

handful of chopped
thyme

½ teaspoon
chopped green
chilli

salt and freshly
ground black
pepper

100 g (3½ oz)
spinach, shredded

4 cherry tomatoes,
quartered

You can play around endlessly with the fillings here and use
pretty much any chopped veg you like – mushrooms, peppers
(bell peppers), courgette (zucchini), broccoli or asparagus. You
can leave out the bacon, and maybe swap in some feta, up the
spice with a bit of harissa or go crazy with the herbs. The only
real rule is to make sure you have a good egg-to-extras ratio so
they puff up properly and hold together. And don't overfill the
muffin tray – you need to leave about 1 cm (½ in) or so space
at the top of each well so they don't overflow as they cook.
These are perfect little bites to stash in the freezer too. Leave
them to cool, then wrap them up individually in baking paper
and freeze in an airtight container. Take them out the night
before eating and let them defrost in the fridge before warming
through in the oven.

Preheat the oven to 180°C (350°F/Gas mark 4).

Dry-fry the bacon in a frying pan over a low heat, letting the low,
slow heat render any fat from the bacon. Cook it through for
about 5 minutes, until it's slightly browned and a little bit crispy.

Meanwhile, whisk the eggs with lots of freshly chopped thyme,
chilli, salt and black pepper. Stir through the shredded spinach.

Divide the eggy mixture between 6 holes in a non-stick muffin
tray and divide the tomato and bacon pieces among them.
(On non-fast days you can also shower them with a delicious
snowstorm of grated Parmesan cheese or feta.)

Bake in the oven for 15–20 minutes, until they have puffed up
and are golden on top. Let them cool a little bit in their trays
before eating.

# Watermelon & Lime Crush

**SERVES 2**

400 g (14 oz/
3 cups) watermelon
chunks*

juice of 1 lime

10 mint leaves

2 mugs of ice

If you're weighting your calories later on in the day, then this is a refreshing, uplifting, better-than-a-cup-of-coffee way to wake up your morning. It tastes like a holiday and will keep you hydrated. Watermelon is one of those fruits we just don't eat enough of! You'll start off your fast day with a smile.

Put all the ingredients in a blender and blitz until smooth. It will have a granita-type texture at first – not totally liquid like a smoothie – so maybe start off eating it with a spoon. It will quickly melt into the most refreshing drink you've ever tasted.

* Watermelon can be a faff to prepare so, although not cheap, you can save yourself a ton of time by buying those packs of pre-prepared cubes.

# A Rainbow of Juices

**EACH MAKES 1**
glass (just double
up if you're
making more!)

Juices shouldn't replace actual meals, but when you're fasting, they can provide tasty shots of colourful vitamins to keep you going and make sure you're getting lots of good nutrients, even if you are eating less. Wash all the fruit and veg well before juicing. I like to blend my juices with ice afterwards too. It makes them feel more substantial, but also makes them taste less intense. And pour a little water through the juicer when it's nearly done, just so you make sure you get all the juices out and into your drink.

## Red

Juice 1 small carrot, 1 beetroot (beet), 3 radishes and 1 small apple. This is a brightly coloured, sweet but earthy juice to get your day going.

## Orange

Juice 2 carrots, a 1 cm (½ in) piece peeled, fresh turmeric, a 2 cm (¾ in) piece peeled ginger, 1 apple and ½ cucumber. Turmeric is a powerful ingredient that has many health-giving properties.

## Yellow

Peel and chunk a 150 g (5 oz) pineapple, then juice with 1 apple. Squeeze in the juice from ½ lemon. This one is quite sweet, so I sometimes stir in a pinch of cayenne pepper.

# Green

A basic green juice that ticks all the right boxes. Juice ½ cucumber, 1 apple, 2 handfuls of greens – such as kale, spinach or chard – with 2 small celery stalks and ½ lime, peel and all. You don't have to juice the peel as well, but I like the extra flavour it brings.

# Purple

Juiced cabbage leaves can get a bit of getting used to, but their amazing colour is hard to beat. For this vaguely goth drink, juice 2 red cabbage leaves, 2 celery stalks, 1 apple and a 2 cm (¾ in) piece peeled ginger.

# Rye Slices

MAKES 1 slice
each

Rye bread is so much more filling than regular white or even regular wholegrain bread. It's packed with fibre and has a lower GI, so you'll keep those blood sugar levels on an even keel. These slices are based on a slice of rye bread coming in at 100 calories. You can buy rye breads ready-sliced at roughly this calorie count, which makes the whole process so much easier. Although these make a great breakfast, you can really eat them any time of day when you need a low-calorie flavour hit.

## Smoked Salmon, Cream Cheese & Cucumber

Spread the rye bread with 1 tablespoon low-fat cream cheese and top with 25 g (1 oz) peeled cucumber slices and 25 g (1 oz) smoked salmon. Squeeze over a little lemon juice and season with black pepper.

## Harissa Hard-Boiled Egg

Hard-boil 1 small egg. Cool and peel, then chop. Mix with ½ teaspoon harissa paste, 1 teaspoon low-fat Greek-style yoghurt and a squeeze of lemon juice. Spread over the rye bread and season with black pepper and some coriander (cilantro) leaves.

## Hard-Boiled Egg with Tomato & Capers

Hard-boil 1 small egg. Cool and peel, then slice. Spread the rye bread with 1 teaspoon Dijon mustard and top with 1 small tomato, sliced, and the egg slices. Scatter over 1 teaspoon capers and 1 teaspoon chopped red onion.

## Almond Butter & Grapes

/185/

Spread the rye bread with 2 teaspoons smooth almond butter and 5 sliced grapes.

## Ricotta & Strawberries

/143/

Spread the rye bread with 30 g (1 oz) fresh ricotta and top with 3 small strawberries, sliced. Sprinkle with a little cinnamon.

## Tahini & Cucumber

/135/

Spread the rye bread with 1 teaspoon tahini. Mix 30 g (1 oz) very fine slices of peeled cucumber with lime juice and chopped mint leaves and pile on top. Scatter over some chilli flakes.

## Goat's Cheese & Radish

/190/

Spread the rye bread with 30 g (1 oz) soft goat's cheese. Top with 4 sliced radishes, and ¼ sliced medium pear, then sprinkle with 2 tablespoons sprouted seeds.

## Pea & Lemon

/150/

Boil 65 g (2 oz/¾ cup) frozen peas for a couple of minutes. Drain and mash with the grated zest and juice of ½ lemon and a few chopped mint leaves. Spread over the rye bread and top with lots of freshly ground black pepper.

/+20/

A shower of grated Parmesan cheese makes this a luxurious start to the day.

# 100-Calorie Smoothie Pouches

EACH SMOOTHIE
MAKES 1 pouch

One of the main rules for success when following the 5:2 is to be PREPARED. And also to keep things interesting so you don't get bored munching on the same things every day. These smoothie pouches answer both of these needs, and are great to have stashed in the freezer: no need to defrost, just whizz them up in your blender with your choice of milk or other liquids and you'll have a thick and creamy, deliciously fruity start to the day.

Remember that whatever milk you use will obviously add extra calories, so keep an eye on that – probably not a day for full fat! I usually make these with 150 ml (5 fl oz/⅔ cup) unsweetened almond milk (20 calories) and a splash or two of water to loosen everything up. But they are also good with coconut water. I use 100 ml (3½ fl oz/½ cup) and make up the rest with plain water (32 calories). These smoothie pouches are also great because you don't have to eat a WHOLE mango all in one day – although that's not too tricky – you can divide it between several freezer bags, spread out the joy and avoid waste. It's a great way to use up whatever bits of fruit you have lurking in your fruit bowl.

You can use standard freezer bags but try and get as much air out of the bags as possible when you pack them up.

## Good Morning

For a well-balanced start to the day, combine ⅓ chopped banana with 40 g (1½ oz/¼ cup) blackberries and 120 g (4 oz/2½ cups) spinach in a pouch. Blend with milk or coconut water and ice.

# Detox

Since you're already doing so well by actually following the 5:2, why not score extra points with this detox smoothie? Pack up 20 g (¾ oz/⅔ cup) fresh coriander (cilantro), a 2 cm (¾ in) piece peeled and chopped ginger, 120 g (4 oz/2½ cups) spinach, 100 g (3½ oz) sliced courgette (zucchini) and 50 g (2 oz) fresh, peeled and chopped pineapple. Blend with milk or coconut water, ice and 4 or 5 fresh mint leaves.

# Banana, Strawberry & Peanut Butter

A classic fruit pouch but with an extra dose of deliciousness to help you through those tough dieting days. Pack up ⅓ chopped banana and 30 g (1 oz/¼ cup) strawberries. Blend with milk or coconut water and 1 teaspoon peanut butter for a smoothie that feels a bit naughty, but has an extra helping of protein to keep you feeling full.

# Tropical Island, Please

If only life was always as simple and sweet as this. Pack up 85 g (3 oz/¼ cup) peeled and chopped mango and 1 peeled and chopped kiwi in a pouch. Then blend with milk or coconut water, some ice and 4 or 5 fresh mint leaves. This one is particularly good made with coconut water for an extra boost of sunshine.

# All the Berries

A simple win-win smoothie. Combine 75 g (2½ oz/½ cup) strawberries, 30 g (1 oz/¼ cup) blueberries and 40 g (1½ oz/ ¼ cup) blackberries in a pack. Blend with milk or coconut water, 4 or 5 fresh mint leaves and a squeeze of lime juice.

# Matcha Green Tea & Peach

You don't need to use matcha green tea powder in this as the banana and peach are delish on their own, but it does make it an amazing colour and has all those green tea antioxidants! Pack up ⅓ chopped banana and 100 g (3½ oz) chopped peach. Blend with milk or coconut water, ½ teaspoon matcha powder, ice and a squeeze of lime.

# Grilled Pineapple
## with Honey & Mint

SERVES 2

4 tinned pineapple rings or 140 g (5 oz/1 cup) pineapple wedges

2 teaspoons honey

pinch of chilli flakes (optional)

60 g (2 oz/¼ cup) plain yoghurt

chopped mint, to garnish

zest of ½ lime, to garnish

One for the sweet-toothed fasters out there! Chilli flakes may seem a bit unbreakfasty, but the fiery punch really helps balance the sweetness – you can, of course, leave them out if you prefer. The mint and yoghurt are cooling and refreshing and the lime zest adds a final flourish of flavour.

Preheat the grill to high. Line a baking tray with foil and place the pineapple pieces on top. Grill the pineapple on one side for about 4 minutes until just starting to brown and caramelise.

Flip the pineapple over and brush with the honey. Return to the grill for another 5 minutes until brown and crispy round the edges.

Plate the pineapple and scatter over the chilli flakes, if using. Serve with the cooling yoghurt and garnish with the chopped mint and lime zest.

# Turkish-Style Baked Eggs

**SERVES 2**

1 spring onion (scallion), finely chopped

1 teaspoon olive oil

20 g (¾ oz/⅔ cup) coriander (cilantro), finely chopped

2 cherry tomatoes, chopped

2 tablespoons plain yoghurt

pinch of chilli flakes

pinch of ground cumin

freshly ground black pepper

2 small eggs

Part of the secret to successful fast days is to make it feel like you've eaten a fully satisfying meal. And one of the ways to do this is to bring strong flavours into your food. These Turkish-style eggs use coriander (cilantro) as a main component, instead of a final garnish, which provides a really earthy taste. If the flavour is too intense for you, you can use chopped spinach instead. You can prep these the night before and then crack in the egg and spoon over the yoghurt in the morning.

Preheat the oven to 200°C (400°F/Gas mark 6).

Fry the spring onion in the oil in a frying pan for a couple of minutes, just to soften them. Divide between two ramekins and use the oil to grease the sides.

Keep the pan over a low heat and add the chopped coriander. Stir it around for no more than 1 minute, just so it wilts. Spoon into the ramekins. Top with the chopped cherry tomato.

Mix the yoghurt with the chilli, cumin and some black pepper.

Crack an egg into each ramekin and spoon over the spiced yoghurt mixture.

Cook in the oven for 10 minutes until the white is cooked through and the yolk is cooked to your liking.

# Power Smoothie

MAKES 2 glasses

1 medium banana, chopped

150 g (5 oz/¾ cup) frozen cherries

400 ml (13 fl oz/1¾ cups) unsweetened almond milk

20 g (¾ oz/¼ cup) oats

5 mint leaves

¼ teaspoon maca powder (optional)

Introducing oats to your regular smoothie routine will bring it new levels of extreme creaminess. Oats are, of course, also an excellent choice on fast days. Replacing some of the fruit in your usual smoothies with oats will help level out some of those sugar spikes that can lead to hungriness later on. You can obviously use fresh cherries instead of frozen here (or anything else you fancy – see pages 39–41 for more smoothie ideas), but frozen fruits give a thicker texture and an ice-cold smoothie is ridiculously refreshing. You don't have to use nut milk either – regular dairy milk is great here, or add a tablespoon of yoghurt if you have the calories to spare. The maca powder gives it all a malty flavour, but leave it out if it's not your thing.

Blitz everything in a blender until smooth and creamy. Easy!

# Dragon Fruit Smoothie Bowl

**SERVES 1**

*For the smoothie*

50 g (2 oz/¼ cup) low-fat Greek-style yoghurt (coconut flavour is good!)

80 g (3 oz) pink-fleshed dragon fruit

100 g (3½ oz) banana, chopped (preferably frozen)

100 ml (3½ fl oz/ ½ cup) unsweetened almond milk

4 mint leaves

*Toppings*

60 g (2 oz) pink-fleshed dragon fruit, scooped into tiny balls with a melon baller, or just chopped

½ kiwi, peeled and chopped

40 g (1½ oz) papaya, peeled and chopped

½ teaspoon poppy seeds

mint leaves

Smoothie bowls are big business these days. As well as being pretty – and slower to gulp down than a regular smoothie in a glass – they are also a great way of piling up all sorts of goodness into one delicious place. The basic premise is to make a smoothie, pour it into a bowl and then add toppings. You can top them with seeds, nuts, granola, fresh and dried fruit, cacao powder, chia seeds, cereal, you can drizzle them with honey, nut butter, maple syrup... you can literally add whatever you feel like (or have lurking in your cupboards). You can also use the smoothie recipes on pages 39–41 and add your favourite toppings – just keep an eye on calories, of course. Spend some time making them look like mini works of art, and they'll be suitable for your Instagram fans, too.

Dragon fruits are expensive, so this is not one for every day, but when you're fasting sometimes you need a treat. And they are a great source of protein and vitamin C. You can get dragon fruit with pink or white flesh, but obviously go for the pink one when you can for maximum wow factor. Frozen dragon fruit is much cheaper if you can find it. If you can't find dragon fruit, then kiwi fruit makes a brilliant substitue – and conveniently has roughly the same amount of calories, gram for gram. Leave off the toppings to save yourself 75 calories. Or only top with the dragon fruit, at 35 calories.

Blend the ingredients for the smoothie. You're eating this with a spoon so keep it quite thick, like thick yoghurt or slightly melted ice cream. Pour into a bowl.

Arrange the toppings beautifully on top – or just pile them on if no one is looking.

# Kale with Bacon

SERVES 2

120 g (4 oz) lean
cut/low-fat bacon,
finely chopped

scrape of coconut
oil

200 g (7 oz/3 cups)
trimmed, chopped
kale (remove any
woody hard bits)

*For the dressing*

1½ tablespoons
wholegrain
mustard

1 teaspoon apple
cider vinegar

freshly ground
black pepper

This contains all the elements of a good fast-day meal. It has strong flavours from the mustard dressing, which makes you feel like you've eaten something really tasty. The kale is full of fibre to fill you up. And the bacon feels just a little bit naughty for a diet day, so you don't feel like you've missed out on all the fun.

You can also top the kale with a small poached egg for an extra protein hit. This will add about 65 calories per serving. Bring the water to the boil while you're cooking the bacon and then turn it down, drop in the egg and simmer until everything is ready.

Put the bacon into a deep saucepan over a low heat. You want it to gently render out the fat so it can cook in it. Fry for 5–10 minutes until it's starting to look cooked – it won't be crisp. At the end, add a tiny scrape of coconut oil to help crisp it up – or add it sooner if the pan is looking very dry.

Add the washed kale and stir it into the bacony goodness. Pop on the lid so it steams. Keep stirring every so often as it softens up so it doesn't stick, cooks evenly and gets coated in the tasty bacon flavours. It will take about 10 minutes.

Meanwhile, whisk together the ingredients for the dressing with a splash of water.

When the bacon and kale are ready (don't let the kale wilt down too much) and while it is all still in the pan, toss through the mustard dressing. Cook with the lid off for just a few seconds to evaporate some of the liquid – you don't want it to be soggy – then serve!

# Overnight Oat Pots

**MAKES 2 pots**

80 g (3 oz/¾ cup) oats

2 teaspoons ground cinnamon

300 ml (10 fl oz/1¼ cups) unsweetened almond milk

2 teaspoons honey

1 large apple

100 g (3½ oz/ ¾ cup) blackberries

These are so filling – the oats will keep you going for hours, plus the apple and berries provide lots of fibre and vitamins. It tastes a little bit like an apple and blackberry crumble . . . pudding for breakfast!

This is also one you can easily adapt. Try it with maple syrup instead of the honey and top with other berries – blueberries, strawberries and raspberries – or even a bit of banana, but just keep an eye on the calories. The berries here are about 22 calories. If you top with banana, you won't need the honey as the banana is already sweet, so you can save yourself some calories there. You can, of course, use other types of milk – coconut, dairy and hemp milk are all delicious. Chopped nuts are also great for adding a satisfying crunch. You can easily leave out the cinnamon if it's not your thing, but it's good for stabilising blood sugar levels to keep you on an even keel.

Divide the oats between two bowls or pots. Divide the cinnamon between them, then stir half the milk and honey into each one. Peel, core and grate the apple, then stir it into the oat mixture. Cover and chill in the fridge overnight.

In the morning, stir through the berries.

# Quinoa Porridge

SERVES 1

30 g (1 oz/¼ cup)
white or red quinoa
(or a mixture)

155 ml (5 fl oz/
½ cup) almond
milk

2 teaspoons vanilla
extract

1 tablespoon
pistachios,
chopped

1 teaspoon honey

50 g (2 oz/⅓ cup)
strawberries,
chopped

Eat a comforting bowl of porridge (oatmeal) in the morning, especially one as pretty as this, and you can tackle pretty much anything that comes your way! Quinoa is a good source of protein and fibre to fill you up. Top the porridge with all kinds of goodies – chopped nuts, fresh fruit, honey, maple syrup, coconut flakes – just keep an eye on the calories, of course. For a lighter version, try cooking the quinoa in coconut water. Double up the batch if you're cooking for more people or make the porridge the night before and reheat it.

Put the quinoa, milk and vanilla in a small saucepan and cook over a gentle heat for about 20 minutes, stirring often, until the quinoa is cooked through and creamy. If it looks like it's drying out, add a little water. Don't let the nut milk boil; just let it simmer quietly.

When the quinoa is the consistency you like, remove from the heat and stir through the chopped pistachios, honey and strawberries.

# Fig, Apricot & Pistachio Granola

**MAKES 7 servings**
(a week's supply)

1 apple, peeled and cored

200 g (7 oz/2 cups) oats

1 teaspoon ground cinnamon

pinch of salt

2 tablespoons maple syrup

1 teaspoon vanilla extract

5 dried figs, chopped

8 dried apricots, chopped

1 tablespoon almonds, chopped

2 tablespoons pistachios, chopped

+50  50 g (2 oz/¼ cup) plain yoghurt, per serving (optional)

The granola you buy at the supermarket is usually full of added sugars and I find it has a fairly disappointing fruit-to-oat ratio, with the fruit mainly made up of raisins. Making it yourself gives you the opportunity to go wild with your dried fruits! It can be quite high in calories, so keep an eye on portion size, but all that oaty, fruity goodness will set your day off with the best of intentions. Serving it with yoghurt, as well as being cooling and refreshing, provides an extra-large protein boost to keep you feeling full all morning – but milk is great too. Almond milk adds an extra nutty layer of flavour.

Preheat the oven to 180°C (350°F/Gas mark 4).

Chop the apple into chunks and place in a small saucepan over a low heat with enough water to cover the pieces. Simmer for 10–15 minutes until soft, then remove from the heat and mash to make a puree.

Mix together the oats, cinnamon and salt, then stir through the apple puree, maple syrup, vanilla, figs, apricots and almonds. Spread out on a baking tray and cook in the oven for about 20 minutes, turning the mixture over gently every so often so it cooks evenly and watching that the fruit doesn't catch and burn. Hopefully you will get some nice clumps of sticky oats – don't break them up as these are what make it so delicious and satisfying when you come to eat it.

When the oats are a nice brown colour around the edges, remove from the oven and stir through the pistachios. Leave to cool before storing in an airtight jar.

Serve, if you like, with yoghurt or milk of your choice.

Lunch

For many fasters, lunch is the first meal of the day. So you have to make it count. The focus here is on fresh, punchy ingredients to excite your senses – lots of aromatics and strong flavours – and lots of high-fibre, high-protein dishes to make you feel full. They are also quick to prepare and almost every one can be made ahead and packed in a lunchbox (so no lurking in the canteen wondering how many calories are in a baked potato). Absolutely none of these are 'diet foods' either – every single one would feel right at home on a non-fast day, too. There's no need to stop eating the foods you love just because you're eating less – enjoying what you eat on fast days will help you stick with it. Keep going, you're halfway there!

# Roast Tomato
# Bloody Mary Soup

SERVES 6

1.4 kg
(3 lb 1 oz)
tomatoes,
quartered

2 garlic cloves,
sliced

1–2 tablespoons
olive oil

2 teaspoons chilli
flakes

salt and freshly
ground black
pepper

2 tablespoons
Worcestershire
sauce

1 teaspoon
horseradish
paste or grated
horseradish root

1 teaspoon apple
cider vinegar

juice of 1 lemon

2 celery stalks,
finely chopped

Who doesn't love a cocktail at lunch?! This spicy soup can be
eaten hot or cold, making it either the perfect winter warmer
or a refreshing bowl on a summer day. You can adjust the
spices and extras to your own tastes. Make a big batch and
freeze it, then defrost and eat straightaway, or reheat gently
until bubbling. On non-fast days (or if you're not at work!),
you can even add a splash of vodka just before serving
(1 tablespoon is about 33 calories . . .).

It's all about the tomatoes here, so make sure you use good
ones. If you're short on time or can't face the faff of roasting
tomatoes, you can use 4 × 400 g (14 oz) tins instead. Cook the
garlic in 1 tablespoon of the oil with the chilli flakes, and drizzle
in the remaining oil when you add all the other flavourings.
It won't be as delicious but will be perfectly acceptable. Think
NYC mixologist versus your local pub.

Preheat the oven to 180°C (350°F/Gas mark 4).

Arrange the tomatoes and garlic on a large roasting tray. Toss in
the olive oil. It won't seem like much, but will be enough. Scatter
over the chilli flakes and season with salt and black pepper. Roast
for 30–40 minutes, until the tomatoes are cooked through and
have shrunk slightly, but are still just about holding their shape.
Hopefully you will have a few sticky, browned skins too.

Remove the tomatoes from the oven and let everything cool a
little bit, then tip into a blender with the garlic and juices, and
blitz until smooth.

Pour into a saucepan and stir in the Worcestershire sauce,
horseradish, vinegar and lemon juice. Bring to a simmer for about
20 minutes until it reaches your desired consistency – it should
be quite thin so it doesn't feel like you're eating pasta sauce.

Season to taste with extra salt and pepper, Worcestershire sauce or lemon juice – this soup is as personal as your Bloody Mary cocktail should be.

Ladle into bowls, pack up for lunch or freeze into portions. Serve with the finely chopped celery on top.

# Asparagus
## with Chopped Egg, Mustard & Capers

**SERVES 1**

1 small egg

200 g (7 oz) trimmed asparagus spears

1 teaspoon Dijon mustard

1 teaspoon capers

squeeze of lemon juice

salt and freshly ground black pepper

It's so important to eat proper food on your fast days. Just because you're eating less on those days, that doesn't mean your meals should be any less delicious. This light lunch – which you can really have at any time of day – feels so much more substantial than the 110 calories that it is, and it's all to do with the balance of textures and flavours, as well as the huge protein hit from every dieter's favourite food – an egg! Obviously you can multiply the amounts to feed more people.

Put the egg in a pan of cold water. Bring to the boil and boil for 8 minutes. After the egg has been boiling for 3 minutes, heat a frying pan over a medium heat and drop in the asparagus. Cover and cook, shaking occasionally – no need to add any water.

When the egg is cooked, peel and chop into a bowl. Keep shaking the asparagus. Mix the chopped egg with the mustard and capers.

Place the asparagus on a plate and squeeze over the lemon. Top with the chopped egg and capers and season with salt and pepper.

# Watermelon & Feta Salad

SERVES 2

400 g (14 oz/
3 cups) watermelon
chunks*

½ small red onion,
very finely sliced

½ small red chilli,
very finely chopped

8 mint leaves,
shredded

90 g (3¼ oz/⅔ cup)
low-fat feta

zest of 1 lime

Watermelon juice provides a sweet dressing for this creamy, salty, crunchy, fresher-than-fresh-tasting salad. This is a great one to pack up and take to work – the red onion will mellow beautifully with the watermelon by lunchtime, and you can't be sad with a bowl of bright red fruit to eat! Better than a shop-bought sandwich any day of the week.

Put the watermelon chunks and juice in a bowl. Gently mix in the onion, chilli and mint leaves. Scatter over the feta and grate the lime zest on top. Ta-dah!

\* Watermelon can
be a faff to prepare
so, although not
cheap, you can
save yourself a ton
of time by buying
those packs of
pre-prepared
cubes.

# Flaked Salmon & Wholewheat Pasta
## with Lime Gremolata

**SERVES 2**

60 g (2 oz/⅔ cup) wholewheat pasta

4 asparagus spears, trimmed and chopped

50 g (2 oz) poached salmon fillet*

freshly ground black pepper

squeeze of lime juice

*For the gremolata*

15 g (½ oz/¾ cup) flat-leaf parsley

zest of 1 lime

1 small garlic clove

Who says you can't eat pasta on a fast day?! You can eat this hot or cold, make it ahead, or make a larger batch to take to work during the week (eat it within a couple of days though, as the herbs won't stay fresh for longer than that). Wholewheat pasta releases energy more slowly than regular pasta, making it a healthier choice, but you can use white pasta if you prefer. The parsley in the gremolata should cancel out any lingering garlic breath, but if you have an important afternoon meeting in the diary, maybe use half a clove or leave the garlic out completely. Gremolata is usually made with lemon zest, but this version is made (perhaps controversially) with lime – you can use either though. Coloured pasta – like beetroot (beet) or sun-dried tomato – looks great with all the bright greens too.

Boil the pasta in salted water according to the packet instructions. In the final minute, drop in the asparagus spears to cook quickly. Drain, but keep back a little of the cooking water.

Meanwhile, make the gremolata. Finely chop the parsley, then grate the lime zest and the garlic over the top. Mix together, chopping through to work the flavours into each other – the easiest way to do this is with a small sharp knife and a fork.

Place the pasta and asparagus in a bowl and gently fold through the gremolata, then flake through the salmon fillet. At this point, see if it could do with loosening up a little. If so, splash in a little of the reserved cooking water.

Season with freshly ground pepper and the lime juice.

* You can buy this already cooked, but you can also easily cook your own by poaching the fish in water (maybe with a slice of lemon) for 15 minutes.

# Aromatic Chicken Noodle Soup

SERVES 2

15 g (½ oz) piece ginger, sliced

2 spikes from a whole star anise

½ red chilli, sliced

1 tablespoon tamari

juice of 1 lime

1 × 100 g (3½ oz) skinless chicken breast

2 bulbs bok choy (pak choy) or 4 baby ones (about 120 g/4 oz), halved

30 g (1 oz/¼ cup) green beans, finely chopped

55 g (2 oz) rice noodles

1 spring onion (scallion), shredded

small bunch of coriander (cilantro), chopped

Sometimes fast days can be tough – especially in the winter. Summer days go hand in hand with lighter salads and frittatas, but when it's cold outside, this noodle soup will warm you up from the inside out. The chicken cooks in the aromatic broth, which is then absorbed by the noodles, making it a perfect one-pot meal. Add more chilli or some dried chilli flakes if you're up for a bit more spice. You can pack this one up for work too: cook ahead without the noodles, then reheat it at the office, popping in the noodles at the same time.

Pour 750 ml (25 fl oz/3 cups) cold water into a saucepan. Add the sliced ginger, star anise, chilli, the tamari and half the lime juice. Bring to a simmer, then drop in the whole chicken breast. Cook for 20 minutes until the chicken is cooked through.

Remove the chicken from the pan. Add the bok choy, beans and noodles to the stock and cook for about 4 minutes while you shred the chicken and divide it between two serving bowls.

Top the chicken with the noodle soup, scatter over the spring onion and coriander leaves and squeeze over the rest of the lime juice.

# Nori Wraps

**MAKES 2 wraps**

2 × nori sheets

½ ripe avocado, mashed

chilli sauce, to drizzle

1 smallish carrot, grated

1 red cabbage leaf, chopped

a few spinach leaves, chopped

a few coriander (cilantro) leaves

+40  6 cooked king prawns (shrimp), chopped (optional)

This recipe is super easy and perfect for packing in a lunchbox to take to work. Seaweed is SO good for you too – it's a great source of iron, protein, fibre and iodine, which is quite hard to find in natural sources, as well as tons of other minerals. Definitely worth swapping these nori wraps for your usual sarnie, even on non-fasting days.

Filling options are endless, but aim for something smooth and a bit sticky (like this mashed avocado or hummus or even tahini paste) to help hold it together, something fresh and crunchy and something with a bit of a kick to make those taste buds happy. Avoid anything too wet though, as it can make the wraps soggy and then they can fall apart.

Spread each nori sheet with the mashed avocado – go right up to the edge as this will help them stick together when you roll them up. Keep the layer thin, as too much can make the wrap soggy and likely to tear. Drizzle over some chilli sauce.

Layer on the grated carrot, cabbage, spinach, coriander and prawns, if using. Then roll up from the edge closest to you, using the avocado edge to help it all hold together. That's it! Pack 'em up and off you go! (You can trim them if you're very concerned with rough edges and slice into pieces or halves.)

# Sweet Potato Hash
## with a 'Fried' Egg

**SERVES 2**

220 g (8 oz/
1¾ cups) grated
sweet potato

pinch of smoked
paprika

1½ tablespoons
chopped thyme

salt and freshly
ground black
pepper

1 teaspoon
coconut oil

2 medium eggs

This dish will bring a giant ray of midday sunshine to your plate. It's packed with flavour and the sweet potato provides lots of lovely fibre to fill you up, while the eggs keep you going all afternoon.

Mix the grated sweet potato with smoked paprika and the thyme and season with salt and pepper.

Melt the coconut oil in a non-stick frying pan over a medium heat.

Add the sweet potato and stir to coat in the oil. Fry for a couple of minutes, then top with a lid and let the sweet potato steam-fry for 10–15 minutes, stirring frequently so it doesn't stick.

When it has cooked through and is pretty soft (but not turning to mush), take off the lid and squish it with the back of the spoon to release some of the liquid and break it down further. Cook for a further 5 minutes or so, squishing and stirring so it doesn't burn or stick. Scoot it to one side, then add a splash of water, crack in the eggs and 'fry' to your liking.

Divide the hash evenly into 2 rings or ramekins if you're feeling fancy – or just pile on to plates – and top with the 'fried' egg and some salt and pepper.

# Vietnamese-ish
# Prawn Salad

SERVES 2

1 medium
courgette (zucchini)

1 medium carrot

1 small cucumber

15 g (½ oz/
¾ cup) mint leaves,
shredded

10 g (½ oz/⅓ cup)
coriander (cilantro)
leaves, shredded

2 spring onions
(scallions),
chopped

1 small red chilli,
chopped

150 g (5 oz)
shelled, deveined,
cooked king
prawns (shrimp)

6 salted roasted
peanuts, crushed

*For the dressing*

juice of 1 lime

2 tablespoons
tamari

2 teaspoons chilli
flakes

1 teaspoon honey

I bet you were wondering when the spiralizer was going to come out! Well, here it is, showcasing its finest skills. This is such a flavourful salad it's hard to believe how few calories it has – the secret is in the powerful dressing – and it smells SO GOOD. Prawns (shrimp) also feel a little bit luxurious, which is just what you need on those days when you're cutting down on calories. This is an easy one to scale up or down, and can be packed up and taken to work – just make sure to keep it chilled.

First start by spiralizing the courgette, carrot and cucumber. If you don't have a spiralizer, then just cut into thin ribbons using a vegetable peeler. Place them all in a large bowl.

Add the shredded mint and coriander leaves to the bowl, then add the spring onion and chilli.

Cut each prawn into three pieces and add to the salad. Give everything a gentle mix so the ingredients are all evenly distributed.

Mix together the ingredients for the dressing with 1 tablespoon water. Pour over the salad and toss to coat. Serve topped with the crushed nuts.

# Kilner Jar Salad

**SERVES 1**

1 tablespoon chopped red onion

50 g (2 oz/¼ cup) tinned chickpeas (garbanzo beans), drained

50 g (2 oz) cucumber, peeled and chopped into small neat cubes

4 cherry tomatoes, halved

40 g (1½ oz) mini mozzarella balls

1 tablespoon sunflower seeds

10 g (½ oz/⅓ cup) basil leaves

15 g (½ oz/⅓ cup) rocket (arugula)

*For the dressing*

juice and zest of ½ lemon

½ tablespoon olive oil

salt and freshly ground black pepper

Even if you can't quite bring yourself to put this in an actual Kilner jar for all the world to see, the idea behind this is still a smart one for making salads ahead of time. By layering all the elements, you keep them apart, so it lessens the chance of soggy lettuce come lunchtime. Of course, you can use whatever you like – just follow the layering rules!

If you don't fancy mozzarella, replace it with 90 g (3 oz) cooked sliced chicken breast, which is the same calorie count, or just leave it out completely. A vegan version of this jar salad will come in at around 185 calories. And you can leave out the oil in the dressing if you like – just use more lemon juice – this will save around 20 calories per serving.

First whisk up the dressing with a splash of water and pour it into the bottom of your jar (or lunchbox).

Next, top with the red onion. Setting it on top of the dressing will help it mellow by midday.

Pile on the chickpeas, chopped cucumber, tomatoes and mini mozzarella balls, then scatter over the sunflower seeds. Finish with the basil and rocket leaves. Seal with a lid.

When you're ready to eat, turn it upside down and give it a bit of shake so the dressing drips down and coats everything. Then uncover and turn out onto a plate. Easy!

# Burrito Bowls

SERVES 2

50 g (2 oz/½ cup)
white or red quinoa
(or a mixture)

80 g (3 oz) tinned
black beans,
drained

½ red (bell)
pepper, deseeded
and cut into strips

½ small red
onion, cut into
strips (roughly the
same size as the
peppers)

80 g (3 oz) tinned
sweetcorn kernels,
drained

½ ripe avocado

juice of 1 lime

small bunch of
coriander (cilantro),
chopped, to serve

+80

*For the chicken*

½ tablespoon olive
oil

1 × 100 g (3½ oz)
skinless chicken
breast, cut into
strips

1 teaspoon smoked
paprika

1 teaspoon chilli
flakes

freshly ground
black pepper

This makes two bowls, but you can easily double up the ingredients to feed the whole family. On non-fast days, or if you have calories to spare, this is great scooped up with nachos or pieces of tortilla, and with a little cheese on top. It's also very well balanced in terms of the right proteins and nutrients. To add a bit more heat, six jalepeño rings on top will only add about 5 calories per serving. For a lower calorie meat-free meal, leave out the chicken. Although this is good when hot, it's equally tasty cooled and packed into a lunchbox.

Put the quinoa in a saucepan with 250 ml (8½ fl oz/1 cup) cold water. Bring to the boil, then reduce the heat to medium-low, cover and simmer for 15 minutes until soft and fluffy, making sure it doesn't dry out. Drain and leave to cool.

Meanwhile, heat the oil in a frying pan over a medium heat and add the chicken strips. Coat in the oil, then scatter over the paprika and chilli flakes and grind over some black pepper. Cook for about 10 minutes, stirring often until golden all over and cooked through.

Heat up the black beans in boiling water for about 7 minutes, then drain.

When the chicken is cooked, transfer it to a plate. Add the red pepper and red onion to the pan, return to the heat and cook in the spicy oils. If it looks dry, add a splash of water. Cook until softened, but not completely soft, then remove from the heat. Mash the avocado with half the lime juice.

To assemble the bowls, divide the quinoa between two serving bowls. Top with the chicken, peppers, onions, black beans and corn. Spoon the mashed avocado on the side, and squeeze over the rest of the lime juice. Scatter over the chopped coriander.

# Kale & Feta
# Baking Tray Eggs

SERVES 4

180 g (6½ oz/
2½ cups) trimmed,
chopped kale,
woody bits
removed

6 small eggs

1 tablespoon milk

salt and freshly
ground black
pepper

1 teaspoon chilli
flakes

salt and freshly
ground black
pepper

90 g (3 oz/⅔ cup)
feta, broken into
chunks

handful of green
salad leaves each,
to serve

This eggy delight is similar to a frittata, except the eggs are cooked in the oven on a baking tray rather than a frying pan. And I think it's a bit easier to make this way. As you're trying to cut down on your fats to keep the calories low, make sure you use a reliably non-stick baking tray, otherwise you'll end up with a kind of scrambled egg meets omelette scenario, which isn't altogether bad, just not quite what we're hoping for. This makes four servings, but it will keep in the fridge for a couple of days and is a perfect pack-up lunch.

Preheat the oven to 180°C (350°F/Gas mark 4). Wilt the kale in a lidded pan with a splash of water for 5–6 minutes; keep stirring it so it wilts evenly. Drain away any excess water.

Whisk the eggs and milk in a bowl and season with salt, pepper and the chilli flakes.

Add the kale and stir to coat, then pour into a baking tray or baking dish. The tray or dish needs to be at least 3 cm (1¼ in) deep, and roughly 20 cm (8 in) square, but it doesn't matter too much – if your dish is larger, you'll just end up with a slightly thinner frittata.

Scatter over the cheese, making sure it's also submerged in the eggy mixture. Bake in the oven for 15–20 minutes, until firm, but still with a slight wobble in the middle, and lightly browned on top.

Leave to cool to at least room temperature, then slice and serve with the salad leaves (or pack up in a lunchbox).

# Wild Rice, Prawn & Mango Salad

**SERVES 1**

25 g (1 oz/⅛ cup) uncooked mixed wild rice

65 g (2¼ oz/⅓ cup) mango, finely chopped

55 g (2 oz) shelled, deveined, cooked king prawns (shrimp), finely chopped

½ small chilli, finely chopped

1 spring onion (scallion), finely chopped

small handful of mixed coriander (cilantro) and mint, finely chopped

2 tablespoons pomegranate seeds

juice and zest of ½ lime

It's hard to believe this salad comes in at 200 calories. Wild rice has a rather unusual nutty taste and slight chewy texture, so every mouthful of this salad is a treat for the senses – silky sweet mango, juicy prawns and a crunchy, sharp-sour pop from the pomegranate seeds. Wild rice is also high in fibre to help keep you feeling full, while the prawns give you a good protein hit. It's a great one to make ahead and pack in a tub for work – just make sure to keep it chilled.

Cook the wild rice in boiling water for about 25 minutes (or according to the packet instructions) until al dente. It will be firmer than regular white or brown rice.

When the rice has cooked, drain and run under cold water to cool it down. Mix in a bowl with the chopped mango, prawns, chilli, spring onion, herbs and pomegranate seeds. Toss together, sprinkle over the lime zest and toss through the lime juice.

210
KCAL

# Fig & Goat's Cheese Salad
## with Reduced Balsamic Dressing

SERVES 1

3 ripe medium figs

20 g (¾ oz) goat's cheese, cut into chunks or slices

1 teaspoon thyme leaves or a couple of sprigs

1 teaspoon Reduced Balsamic dressing (page 23)

It's hard to call this one a recipe since it's really a very quick assembly dish, but sometimes on fast days you don't want to spend long preparing and thinking about food. Pack this in a lunchbox and take it to work – the creamy goat's cheese will seem outrageously inappropriate for a diet day.

Tear or slice the figs into your bowl (or lunchbox). Arrange the cheese over the top and scatter with the thyme leaves. Drizzle over the balsamic dressing and voila! A taste of holidays far away in the sunshine.

# Pokē Bowls

**MAKES 2 bowls**

100 g (3½ oz) very,
very fresh tuna, cut
into chunks

100 g (3½ oz)
cucumber, peeled
and diced

65 g (2 oz) podded
edamame beans

5 radishes, very
finely sliced

40 g (1½ oz)
pickled seaweed
(wakame) or grated
carrot

2 tablespoons
pickled ginger

*For the marinade/
dressing*

1½ tablespoons
tamari

1 teaspoon rice
wine vinegar

1 teaspoon sesame
oil

1 teaspoon black
(or white) sesame
seeds

½ teaspoon very
finely chopped red
chilli

2 spring onions
(scallions), very
finely chopped

a few coriander
(cilantro) leaves

On a recent trip to New York, it became apparent that pokē bowls really were a 'thing'. There were pokē pop-ups literally everywhere. As a sushi-lover, I couldn't get enough of these little bowls of deliciousness. The basics are simple: very fresh raw fish – usually tuna or salmon – with a choice of umami extras: seaweed, avocado, fried shallots and rice were regulars on the pokē bowl circuit. Here's my low-cal interpretation. Make sure your tuna is so fresh you can eat it raw – ask a fishmonger or at the fish counter.

In a shallow bowl, whisk together the ingredients for the marinade/dressing. Add the tuna chunks and leave to marinate for 10 minutes.

Arrange the rest of the salad ingredients in a bowl and top with the fish. Drizzle over the marinade dressing, and serve. You can also make this ahead and pack this into the fridge for a few hours.

# Quinoa, Feta, Pea & Mint Salad
## with Lemon & Chilli

**SERVES 1**

35 g (1¼ oz/ ¼ cup) white or red quinoa (or a mixture)

5 g (¼ oz/about 25) mint leaves, finely shredded

juice and zest of 1 lemon

½ small red chilli, deseeded if preferred, finely chopped

30 g (1 oz/¼ cup) frozen peas, thawed

25 g (1 oz/¼ cup) feta, chopped into small cubes

freshly ground black pepper

Eating on a fast day needn't mean resorting to beige food. Keep your appetite and your eyes sated with this colourful salad that is packed with protein. You can swap in edamame beans instead of the peas if you can get your hands on them, and some chopped spring onion (scallion) is a good addition too – but be aware, of course, that these will affect the calorie count. This is a great salad to make in a big batch to eat throughout the week.

Place the quinoa in a small saucepan with 125 ml (4 fl oz/½ cup) cold water. Bring to the boil over a high heat, then reduce the heat to medium-low, cover and simmer for 15 minutes until soft and fluffy. Keep an eye on the quinoa so it doesn't dry out.

When the quinoa is cooked, drain it well and transfer to a bowl. Gently fold through the mint leaves, so they soften a little in the heat. Squeeze over the lemon juice and mix in the chilli and the thawed peas. Mix through the feta.

Sprinkle over the lemon zest and season with black pepper.

# Thai Beef Salad

**SERVES 2**

½ teaspoon coconut oil

225 g (8 oz) extra lean beef steak

salt and freshly ground black pepper

10 g (½ oz/ ⅓ cup) basil leaves (Thai if possible)

15 g (½ oz/¾ cup) mint leaves

10 g (½ oz/⅓ cup) coriander (cilantro) leaves

40 g (1½ oz/1 cup) rocket (arugula)

1 small cucumber, peeled and cut into ribbons

½ small red onion, finely sliced

100 g (3½ oz/ 1 cup) bean sprouts, trimmed

*For the dressing*

juice of 1 lime

1 tablespoon fish sauce

½ teaspoon soft brown sugar

1 small red chilli, deseeded, finely chopped

This salad is a perfect example of a successful fast-day meal. It has masses of flavour from the dressing and herbs, a gentle spice from the fresh chilli to wake up those taste buds, the beef makes it feel a bit luxurious for a diet day and it is full of crunch and fibre. Plus, you can make it ahead of time – pour over the dressing just before serving so the leaves don't go soggy. #winning.

If you don't eat red meat, or want to save yourself some calories, you can swap the beef for 150 g (5 oz) cooked prawns (shrimps), but no need to cook them in the coconut oil. This will give you a total of just 120 calories. There's a reason prawns are a 5:2-ers go-to.

Grease a non-stick frying pan with the coconut oil. Season the steak on both sides with salt and pepper. Heat the frying pan over a medium-high heat until hot, then add the steak. Cook for about 3 minutes without moving it, then flip it over and cook for a further 2–3 minutes, depending on how thick your steak is and how well done you like it. Remove the steak from the pan and leave to one side to rest and cool for about 5 minutes, while you prepare the salad.

Thoroughly whisk together all the ingredients for the dressing in a small bowl.

Toss together the herbs, rocket, cucumber ribbons, onion and bean sprouts. Add the dressing and toss to coat.

Slice the rested steak diagonally into thin strips. Divide the salad between two bowls and top with the steak. Pour over any leftover dressing lurking in the bottom of the bowl.

Dinner

For most 5:2-ers, eating a proper dinner is the reward for getting through the day. And by saving up those calories it also means you can sit down with the family and all eat together, rather than watching from a distance like a hungry labrador. Most of the recipes in this chapter have been designed so that they can be served up alongside a few 'extras' like rice or a big salad, or some warm fluffy breads. These are obviously not going to make it onto your fasting day plate, but if you're eating with other people then they can have a few sides as well as the main event to bulk up the calories. And it also means you can enjoy these recipes on non-fasting days too! Lots of the recipes in this section can be made ahead and frozen, or pre-prepared and finished off at the last minute – and, as we all know, organisation is one of the main secrets of success on a fast day.

A NOTE TO SAY

A GREAT BIG

# Thank you

Thanks for my lovely Christmas present.

It was very kind of you.

We had a great Christmas and hope you did too.

Love from Annabelle x

Ps. lego was completely new 2 us and it's been awesome fu or Grumbo!

# Sweet Potato
# & Lentil Curry

SERVES 4

1 small onion, chopped

1 garlic clove, chopped

1 teaspoon turmeric

1 teaspoon ground coriander

1 teaspoon cumin seeds

1 teaspoon ground ginger

½ teaspoon chilli flakes

15 g (½ oz) grated ginger

75 g (2½ oz/ ⅓ cup) red lentils

170 g (6 oz) sweet potato, peeled and chopped

1 × 400 g (14 oz) tin chopped tomatoes

50 g (2 oz/1 cup) spinach leaves

*To serve*

1 spring onion (scallion), chopped

5 g (¼ oz/¼ cup) coriander (cilantro)

juice of ½ lemon

Perfect for batch cooking and freezing. If you're going to freeze it, cook it until just before you add the spinach, then cool and freeze in portions. Defrost, warm through thoroughly (you may need a splash of water to loosen it as it heats up), and stir through the spinach just before serving. This is a great one if you're feeding the family as you can serve it with a big pot of rice and breads for everyone else. And if you have any spare calories, a dollop of plain yoghurt is great on the side.

'Fry' the onion and garlic in a deep saucepan in a little water for about 5 minutes, until soft and translucent (they won't colour). Add the spices and grated ginger and stir to coat the onion. Cook for about 30 seconds.

Add the lentils and sweet potato pieces and stir to coat in all the lovely spices. Tip in the tin of tomatoes, then fill up the tin with water and add that to the saucepan. Increase the heat and let it simmer for 15–20 minutes, until the lentils and potato are soft.

Stir through the spinach and let wilt for about 30 seconds, but don't cook for too long otherwise it will turn slimy.

Divide between 4 bowls and top with the chopped spring onion, coriander and a squeeze of lemon juice.

# Courgette Spaghetti
## with Creamy Almond Pesto

SERVES 2

2 courgettes
(zucchini),
spiralized or sliced
into ribbons with a
vegetable peeler

*For the pesto*

2 tablespoons
almonds

½ garlic clove

30 g (1 oz/⅔ cup)
basil

1 tablespoon
grated Parmesan

juice of 1 lemon

salt and freshly
ground black
pepper

a few basil leaves,
to garnish

Ah, our old friend the spiralizer. This is one of those meals that you'll definitely eat even when it's not a fast day. It seems like a very tiny amount of cheese, but it's such a strong flavour that a little goes a very long way. You can also pack this one up for lunch – it's delicious cold on a hot day. Or, for non-fasters, you could serve it with some buttery fried lamb steaks.

Blitz all the pesto ingredients in a mini blender until smooth, then season to taste with salt and pepper. If it needs loosening up a little, mix in a splash of water.

Heat a frying pan (with a lid) over a medium heat and warm through the courgette. Pop the lid on for about 4 minutes, so it steam-cooks and softens a little, but don't let it go soggy. Lift the lid and toss the courgette around every so often so it cooks evenly. Remove the lid and stir through the pesto. Warm through for a minute or so, then serve garnished with basil leaves.

# Greens & Beans Soup

SERVES 4

2 onions, finely chopped

2 celery stalks, finely chopped

1 × 400 g (14 oz) tin cannellini beans, rinsed and drained (240 g drained weight)

salt and freshly ground black pepper

200 g (7 oz/3 cups) kale, trimmed of woody bits and chopped

150 g (5 oz/3 cups) spinach

salt and freshly ground black pepper

20 g (¾ oz) Parmesan

+25 *For the 'croutons'*

18 almonds

1½ tablespoons tamari

Winter is a terrible time for dieting, when all you want to do is tuck into buttery pastry-topped pies and crumbles. But, needs must – and just think of all that Christmas dinner you can eat. This nourishing soup is great to make in bulk and freeze in portions. On non-fast days, serve with crusty bread – or even cheese on toast. Instead of almond 'croutons', you could also fry up some chopped bacon and scatter on top.

In a medium saucepan, 'fry' the onions and celery in a splash of water over a medium heat for about 10 minutes. The onions and celery should be soft and translucent. If it starts to dry out, splash in some more water.

Add the beans and 1 litre (1¾ pints) water. Season with salt and lots of pepper. Bring to a simmer for 10 minutes or so, then add the kale and spinach. Cook for about 5 minutes, until the greens are wilted – but don't overcook as they will become soggy and slimy. Blitz with a hand or jug blender until smooth – if it's too thin for your taste, return to the pan for a few minutes.

Meanwhile, quickly dry-fry the almonds in a pan over a medium-high heat for about a minute. Keep the pan moving so they cook evenly all over. They should darken and smell delicious, but be careful you don't burn them. When they look a few shades darker, splash in the tamari and quickly stir around to coat the almonds – it will bubble up and become a bit sticky. Tip the almonds onto a plate or board and chop them up roughly.

Serve the soup with grated Parmesan and more pepper. Top with the almond 'croutons'. Or cool, portion and freeze. Defrost and reheat thoroughly, then cook the almonds and grate over the Parmesan.

# Prawn Summer Rolls
## with Dipping Sauce

MAKES 4 rolls
(2 rolls and
½ dipping sauce
per serving)

25 g (1 oz) thin dry
rice noodles

4 × 20 cm (8 in)
rice paper
wrappers (spring
roll wrappers)

6 cooked prawns,
peeled, deveined
and halved
lengthways

12 mint leaves,
shredded

2 leaves of Little
Gem or iceberg
lettuce, shredded

½ carrot, sliced into
thin matchsticks

4 radishes,
sliced into thin
matchsticks

¼ cucumber,
peeled, deseeded
and sliced into thin
matchsticks

+21

*For the nuoc cham
dipping sauce*

juice of 1 lime

2 tablespoons fish
sauce

2 teaspoons soft
brown sugar

½ garlic clove,
crushed

1 small red chilli,
deseeded and
finely chopped

Oh. My. Goodness. I literally can't get enough of these things.
They are SO good. They are healthy, crunchy, tasty, fresh,
and the dipping sauce is unbelievably moreish. I think they
may be my favourite things to eat. The soaking and rolling
of the rice paper wraps take a bit of practice, but once you've
mastered that, off you go. Fill with whatever you fancy – here
is my favourite filling. You can leave out the prawns, or swap
for cooked shredded chicken or even avocado. I usually eat two.
Pack them in a box and take the dip in a little pot.

Soak the rice noodles in a bowl of hot water until soft. Drain
the noodles. Make sure you have everything neatly chopped
and ready.

One rice paper at a time, dip it in a bowl of warm water until it
softens slightly – about 5–10 seconds. You don't want it to get
so soft it will fall apart when you roll it, so ensure it keeps its
structure; it will carry on softening when it's out of the water.
Take it out before you think it's ready.

Lay the wrapper on a plate (not a wooden board as the rolls will stick
and it will be a disaster) and place three prawn halves towards one
edge of the wrapper – leave about a 2 cm (¾ in) border at the edge
nearest you. Pile on a quarter of the mint leaves, noodles, lettuce,
carrot, radish and cucumber. Don't try to pack too much in as they
will be tricky to roll up and may split open.

Start rolling from the edge nearest you, and tuck over the ends
as you roll, to keep everything in place. Repeat with the rest of
the wrappers and filling ingredients.

To make the dip, combine all the ingredients in a small bowl.
Taste, and adjust if you think it needs more sugar or lime juice
(this will very slightly alter the calories, but only by a little).

# Chicken, Broccoli & Stelline Soup

SERVES 4

1 tablespoon olive oil

3 spring onions (scallions), chopped

1 garlic clove, chopped

pinch of chilli flakes

1 broccoli head (330 g/11½ oz), broken into small florets– (also chop the stem)

salt and freshly ground black pepper

2 bay leaves

1 × 120 g (4 oz) skinless chicken breast

140 g (5 oz) stelline pasta (or orzo)

small bunch of flat-leaf parsley, chopped

Soup is great, but adding pasta to it makes it feel more like a meal. Stelline (little star-shaped pasta) is also very pretty – and part of getting through a fast day is enjoying what you eat. And, as we all know, we eat first with our eyes and then with our bellies. You can use any type of pasta though, or even rice. If you want to freeze this, take it to the point when you blitz the broccoli – cook the chicken and pasta when you actually want to eat.

Get a couple of pans of water on to boil. Meanwhile, heat the oil in a separate medium-sized saucepan and fry the spring onions, garlic and chilli flakes for 2–3 minutes. Add the broccoli pieces and stir to coat in the garlicky-chilli oil, then pour in 900 ml (1½ pints) water and season with a generous amount of salt and pepper. Simmer for 15–20 minutes, until the broccoli is just tender – poke it with a knife to check.

While the broccoli is cooking, add the bay leaves to one of the pans of boiling water and poach the chicken for 10–15 minutes until cooked through (no pink bits). Transfer to a board or plate and shred.

Add a large pinch of salt to the other pan of boiling water and cook the stelline pasta (or orzo) for 7–8 minutes (check the packet for instructions). Drain well.

When everything is ready, blitz the broccoli soup until very smooth. If it seems a bit thin, then you can return it to the pan for a few minutes. Stir through the pasta. Ladle into bowls and top with the shredded chicken and chopped parsley.

# Chicken, Nectarine, Rocket & Walnut Salad

SERVES 2

1 × 150 g (5 oz) skinless chicken breast

2 sprigs of thyme, plus a few extra leaves to serve

2 deliciously ripe nectarines (270 g /10 oz in total)

35 g (1 oz/1 cup) rocket (arugula)

35 g (1 oz/1 cup) watercress, large pieces broken up and very thick stalks removed

4 walnut halves, lightly crushed

This is a lovely light evening meal that ticks all the 5:2 boxes. It's high in protein to fill you up, the nectarine provides a smooth texture, the lovely juicy dressing feels like a real sweet treat, the rocket and watercress are punchy and fiery and the walnuts give a balancing crunch. Perfect. Leaving out the walnuts will reduce the total calories per portion to 160.

First, cook the chicken. Bring a pan of water to the boil, with a couple of sprigs of thyme in it. Poach the chicken for about 20 minutes until cooked through. Remove and shred the meat.

Meanwhile, stone and slice the nectarines, reserving the juice.

Mix the rocket and watercress together and arrange a pile of leaves on each serving plate. Top with the nectarine and shredded chicken, and pour over the reserved nectarine juice. Scatter over the walnuts and extra thyme leaves.

# Spiced Cauliflower Dhal
## with Fresh Mango Chutney

**SERVES 2**

450 g (1 lb) cauliflower, broken into largish florets

2 teaspoon sumac

2 teaspoon cumin seeds

salt and freshly ground black pepper

*For the dhal*

1 onion (100 g/ 3½ oz), chopped

15 g (½ oz) piece ginger

pinch of chilli flakes

1 teaspoon ground cumin

2 teaspoons ground coriander

1 teaspoon turmeric

freshly ground black pepper

100 g (3½ oz/ ⅓ cup) red lentils

65 g (2 oz/ 1¼ cups) spinach leaves

100 ml (3½ fl oz/ ½ cup) unsweetened almond milk

5 g (¼ oz/¼ cup) fresh coriander (cilantro)

juice of ½ lemon

You can double up the batch of dhal and freeze this – you can cook the cauliflower and freeze that too, but it's better freshly cooked on the day of eating. It will need a little longer cooking time if you are using more ingredients (40–45 minutes should be enough). On non-fast days, use a little coconut oil on the cauliflower and when cooking the onion, and serve with rice and poppadoms or breads if you're feeding the family.

Preheat the oven to 190°C (375°F/Gas mark 5).

Give the cauliflower a wash and while it is still wet, arrange the florets on a baking tray. Scatter over the sumac, cumin seeds, salt and pepper and toss to coat – the water will help the spices stick and will steam the cauliflower a little as it cooks. Cook in the oven for 30–40 minutes; keep an eye on the florets and shuffle them around on the tray so that they cook evenly.

Meanwhile, make a start on the dhal. 'Fry' the onion in a saucepan with a little water over a medium heat for about 8 minutes, until soft and translucent. Be careful that it doesn't get too dry; splash in a little water if needed. Grate in the ginger and add the dry spices. Stir for about 30 seconds, then add the lentils. Stir to coat in the mix, then pour in 450 ml (15 fl oz/2 cups) water. Bring to a bubble, then simmer for about 30 minutes, until the lentils are soft and the liquid has reduced.

While the dhal is cooking, make the mango chutney. Peel and chop the mango – not too small. Slice the spring onions. Combine these with the rest of the chutney ingredients in a small bowl.

**For the chutney**

50 g (2 oz) mango

1 spring onion (scallion)

juice of ½ lime

1 teaspoon chopped red chilli

When the lentils are cooked, stir through the spinach leaves. Let them wilt for about 1 minute, but don't overcook as they can get a bit slimy. Stir through the almond milk and coriander.

Serve the dhal with a squeeze of lemon juice, the roasted cauliflower on top and the fresh mango chutney on the side.

# Shakshuka

**SERVES 2**

2 small onions, finely chopped

1 teaspoon turmeric

1 teaspoon ground ginger

1 teaspoon ground cumin

1 teaspoon ground coriander

pinch of chilli flakes

½ red chilli, finely chopped (optional)

freshly ground black pepper

2 × 400 g (14 oz) tins peeled plum tomatoes

2 cm (¾ in) piece ginger

200 g (7 oz/4 cups) spinach leaves

2 medium eggs

small handful of coriander (cilantro), chopped

Obviously if you are on a feast day you can cook the onions in a delicious amount of olive oil, but you do have to make *some* sacrifices on fast days. Yes, this uses a lot of spices, but these are just the kinds of ingredients that will make your fasting days so much more enjoyable – they're not expensive and they provide so much flavour that you won't realise you're eating so few calories.

Alternatively, you can also use 1 quantity of the Basic Tomato Sauce on page 21 and add the spices and chilli straight to it, bring to a simmer for 10–15 minutes and then pick up the recipe when you add the ginger (leaving out the onions and tinned tomatoes here if you use the basic sauce).

In a deep saucepan (about 20 cm/8 in across) 'fry' the chopped onion in a little water and a little of the juice from the tomatoes for about 5 minutes over a medium heat. The onions should become soft and translucent.

Add the spices and chopped chilli (if using) and season with pepper, then coat the onion in the spicy mix. Stir gently for about 30 seconds, but absolutely do not let the spices burn.

Turn up the heat to medium-high, mix in the tinned tomatoes and break down any that are still whole with a wooden spoon. When they are bubbling, reduce the heat and let simmer for 20–25 minutes until it is thickened. (On non-fast days you can also stir in a generous dollop of tomato purée.) You want it to be quite thick and without much obvious liquid on the surface.

When it's almost as thick as you'd like to eat it, but not quite, grate in the ginger (I like to keep this as fresh as possible for maximum fire) and stir in the spinach leaves. It may seem like a lot of spinach and you'll probably have to load it in in a couple of batches while the leaves wilt. As soon as they have wilted, stir through.

Make a couple of wells in the mixture and crack an egg into each one. Pop on a lid and let the eggs cook for about 10 minutes, depending on how well done you like them. You'll need to do a stirring manoeuvre every so often so that the sauce doesn't stick to the bottom of the pan – sort of stirring *under* the eggs while trying not to disturb them in their nests.

Ladle into bowls and scatter over the fresh coriander. (On non-fast days, some feta is delicious crumbled on top too.)

# Cannellini Bean & Chorizo Stew

SERVES 2

12 g (½ oz) chorizo, skin removed and chopped

1 small red onion, chopped

1 garlic clove, chopped

230 g (8 oz) drained weight tinned cannellini beans

1 × 400 g (14 oz) tin chopped tomatoes

salt and freshly ground black pepper

1 teaspoon apple cider vinegar

1 tablespoon chopped flat-leaf parsley, to garnish

1 teaspoon lemon zest, to garnish

If you have some of the Basic Tomato Sauce (page 21) for this in the freezer, you can use it here! Defrost 1 quantity of the sauce, fry the chopped chorizo for a couple of minutes, then add the sauce and beans and cook as the rest of the recipe (leaving out the onion, garlics and chopped tomatoes). You can also freeze the stew – but not if you've already defrosted the tomato sauce. Defrost and heat through thoroughly. For non-fasters, serve with lots of crusty bread.

Put the chopped chorizo in a saucepan over a low heat and cook for about 2 minutes, just until the fat starts to come out. Add the onion and garlic and let them cook in the spicy oil for about 5 minutes.

When they are soft and a little browned, add the beans and stir for about 30 seconds to coat them in the lovely flavours.

Add the tinned tomatoes and let it simmer gently for 20–25 minutes until the beans soften and the sauce thickens.

Season with salt and pepper and stir in the vinegar. Simmer for a couple more minutes, then serve garnished with a little chopped parsley and a grating of lemon zest.

# Fresh Herb, Asparagus & Feta Omelette

SERVES 1

115 g (4 oz) trimmed asparagus

a couple of squeezes of lime juice and a grating of lime zest

2 medium eggs

a few sprigs of fresh thyme

freshly ground black pepper

scrape of coconut oil

10 g (½ oz) feta, crumbled

a few fresh basil and mint leaves, chopped, to serve

This is more of a thin, Chinese-style pancake of an omelette to wrap around your asparagus filling than a standard fluffy omelette. If you use a smaller pan you can, of course, make a thicker, puffier version but you'll need to cook it for a little longer. Whichever option you choose, you'll need a very good non-stick pan (with a lid) for this – that's how you can get away with using so little fat. It may not seem like much cheese, but it's honestly just enough to give you a salty, luscious hit to offset the rich eggs and fresh asparagus. Don't leave out the lime zest at the end – extra flavour to get your taste buds going. This is definitely one you'll find yourself eating on feast days!

Put the asparagus in a frying pan with a splash of water and put the lid on. Cook for about 10 minutes, shaking the pan around every so often so it doesn't stick or dry out. When it is pretty soft, take the lid off and let the water evaporate. Squeeze over some lime juice, give them a shake, and then remove the asparagus from the pan and set to one side.

Meanwhile, whisk the eggs with a generous trimming of thyme and black pepper.

Off the heat, wipe the pan with kitchen towel and then wipe with a small amount of coconut oil. Return to the heat. When the oil has melted, pour in the beaten eggs and swirl around to coat the bottom of the pan. Use a spatula to break up the base so the uncooked egg can flow in. When it's looking almost cooked through – but don't let it get too dry – pile the asparagus up on one half, then top with crumbled feta and the fresh basil and mint leaves. Flip the other side of the omelette over to cover the top and let it all warm through for a minute or so.

Grate over a little lime zest– and an extra squeeze of juice if you like. Slide onto a plate and serve!

# Sticky-Glazed Salmon Skewers

SERVES 2

1 × 160 g (5½ oz) skinless salmon fillet, cut into 2 cm (¾ in) chunks

*For the glaze*

1½ tablespoons tamari

1 teaspoon honey

1 green or red chilli

1 garlic clove

15 g (½ oz) piece ginger

2 spring onions (scallions), shredded

*For the salad*

1 small cucumber

2 large radishes

Powerful flavours make fast-day eating a pleasure. In this dish, every mouthful is a satisfying combination of sweet and hot, with a refreshing crunchy salad for balance. For non-fasters, serve with some simply cooked rice. You can even pack up a few freezer bags with portions of uncooked fish in the marinade and freeze them – then let them defrost thoroughly in the fridge overnight before cooking as below.

Blitz the ingredients for the glaze (apart from the spring onion) in a mini blender, adding a splash of warm water to loosen it and help melt the honey.

Place the chunks of salmon in a shallow bowl, pour over the glaze and combine with the shredded spring onion. Leave to marinate for about 10 minutes or overnight.

Heat a non-stick frying pan (with a lid) over a medium-high heat. Don't let it get too hot; you're not going to be cooking the salmon with any fat so you don't want it to get too hot as the fish will stick. Tip in the salmon and the marinade and pop the lid on the frying pan. Steam-fry for about 8 minutes, moving the fish around occasionally and turning the pieces over gently so they cook all over and almost all the way through. The sauce should become lovely and sticky too. When the fish is cooked, remove the lid and let the sauce bubble away a little bit and the edges of the fish crispen slightly.

While the fish is cooking, make the salad. Use a vegetable peeler to cut ribbons from the cucumber, discarding the seeded bit in the middle. Peel ribbons from the radishes too. Divide between the serving bowls.

Serve the salmon with the salad, drizzling over any juices from the pan.

DINNER

# Baked White Fish
## with Nutty-Herb-Lemon Crust and A Fennel & Clementine Salad

SERVES 2

2 × 125 g (4 oz) skinless, boneless sustainably sourced cod fillets (or haddock or monkfish)

juice of ½ lemon and zest of 1 lemon

35 g (1 oz/¼ cup) almonds, finely chopped

2 teaspoons olive oil

2 tablespoons chopped flat-leaf parsley

salt and freshly ground black pepper

*For the salad*

1 small fennel bulb

1 clementine

All the nuts make this crunchy topping beautifully satisfying, and the clementine and fennel salad is light and refreshing. A great combination of textures. You can use monkfish or haddock instead – just check the calories match up and adjust the quantity of fish accordingly. Each 125 g (4 oz) skinless, boneless cod fillet has around 90 calories.

Preheat the oven to 180°C (350°F/Gas mark 4).

Line a baking tray with foil and place the fish fillets on top. In a small bowl, combine the lemon juice and zest, almonds, olive oil and parsley. Season with salt and pepper. Divide between the fish and press into the top surface. Bake in the oven for about 15 minutes, until the fish is cooked through.

While the fish is cooking, finely slice the fennel, including the fronds. Pare and segment the clementine, reserving the juice, and chop into small pieces. Combine the fennel and clementine.

Serve the fish with the crunchy fresh salad. Pour over any salady juices.

# Beef & Lentil Chilli

**MAKES** 8 portions

2 tablespoons olive oil

1 large carrot, finely chopped

1 large onion, finely chopped

500 g (1 lb 2 oz) 5% fat minced (ground) beef

1 red (bell) pepper, deseeded and finely chopped

salt and freshly ground black pepper

1 teaspoon chilli flakes

1 teaspoon ground coriander

1 teaspoon ground cumin

1 teaspoon freshly grated ginger

2 × 400 g (14 oz) tins chopped tomatoes

250 g (9 oz/ 1⅓ cups) dry lentils (green lentils are good here as they hold their shape better)

lots of fresh coriander (cilantro), to serve

lime juice, to serve

Amazingly, 5 per cent fat minced (ground) beef has about the same calories as 2 per cent fat minced (ground) turkey, so you can easily substitute for the other. Turkey is very underrated and great value. Personally, though, I love a hearty beef chilli. Forego the sour cream and guac on a fast day and top with lots of fresh coriander and lime juice instead. I've based this around a standard 500 g (1 lb 2 oz) pack of minced beef, which is why it makes so many portions, but it is an excellent one to bulk cook and then freeze. Defrost thoroughly before reheating. Lentils replace the need for rice, but on hungry non-fast days, or for the rest of the family, you can serve with some brown rice.

Heat the oil in a large, deep saucepan over a medium heat and fry the carrot and onion for about 10 minutes, until soft.

Stir in the beef and red pepper, and cook, stirring, for about 10 minutes, until the beef is no longer pink and has some browned, crispy bits. The pepper should also be quite soft.

Season with salt and pepper, then stir in the spices and ginger and cook for about 30 seconds. Add the chopped tomatoes, lentils and 400 ml (13 fl oz/1¾ cups) water. Bring to a boil, then reduce the heat and simmer for 30 minutes, until the lentils are soft and the liquid has reduced. If it's still a bit liquidy, turn up the heat and let it bubble away for a couple of minutes.

Serve with plenty of chopped coriander and a generous squeeze of lime juice.

# Courgette, Mushroom & Sun-Dried Tomato Tortilla Pizzas

MAKES 2 pizzas

½ tablespoon olive oil (or use some of the oil from the sun-dried tomatoes)

1 courgette (zucchini), finely sliced

pinch of chilli flakes (optional)

1 teaspoon dried rosemary

½ × quantity Basic Tomato Sauce (see page 21) (make sure it has a good, thick consistency – reduce it in a pan if it looks a little thin)

2 × gluten-free wraps

80 g (3 oz) mushrooms, sliced

15 g (½ oz) sun-dried tomatoes in oil (about 4), drained

40 g (1½ oz) feta cheese

12 basil leaves, roughly torn

The bases of these little pizza treats are made from gluten-free wraps. The wraps come in at around 100 calories each. But you don't have to go gluten-free; any wrap will do – a spinach wrap or a wholemeal wrap makes a nice change and you can get some good rectangular ones too. You then spread on some Basic Tomato Sauce (see page 21) and top with your favourite toppings. There are two rules: 1 – don't spread on too much sauce as it will go soggy, and 2 – don't pile up the toppings as they won't cook properly and this will also make them soggy. Think Napoli-style with your pizzas – thin and crispy and simple toppings.

To reduce the calories, omit the courgette (zucchini), and therefore the oil, and just go with a simple mushroom and sun-dried tomato pizza. This will save you 40 calories. Or you could skip the feta to save 55 calories.

Preheat the oven to 180°C (350°F/Gas mark 4) and put two baking trays in the oven to heat up.

Heat the oil in a frying pan and fry the courgette slices with the chilli (if using) and rosemary for 5–10 minutes until they are a little browned.

Take the trays out of the oven and place a wrap on each one. Spread half the tomato sauce across each of the wraps, leaving a border all the way round.

Top the pizzas with the cooked courgette, sliced mushrooms and chopped sun-dried tomato. Crumble over the feta and scatter over the basil leaves. Cook for 10 minutes until the mushrooms and sauce are cooked and the edges are a little browned and crispy. The baking tray should help crisp up the base.

# Butternut Squash Jewelled Quinoa Salad

**SERVES 2**

300 g (10½ oz/ 2 cups) peeled and cubed butternut squash

1 tablespoon olive oil

1 tablespoon sumac

salt and freshly ground black pepper

60 g (2 oz/½ cup) white or red quinoa

about 25 mint leaves

about 25 coriander (cilantro) leaves

10 pistachio nuts

45 g (1½ oz/ ¼ cup) pomegranate seeds

2 tablespoons dried cranberries

½ small red chilli, chopped and deseeded

zest of 1 orange

*For the dressing*

juice of 1 orange (about 4 tablespoons)

1 teaspoon wholegrain mustard

You can't beat a fancy jewelled salad like this. Eat it while it's warm, or make ahead of time and store it in the fridge to eat cold (it will keep for a day). It's a generous portion so, if you're weighting your calories more evenly throughout the day, make the whole lot but then only serve up half. It will keep in the fridge overnight so you can take any leftovers for lunch.

Preheat the oven to 180°C (350°F/Gas mark 4).

Spread out the cubes of butternut squash on a baking tray. Drizzle over the olive oil and toss to coat. Scatter over the sumac and season with salt and pepper. Roast for 35–40 minutes until soft and a little bit sticky. Turn over the pieces regularly so they cook evenly. Remove from the oven and leave to cool a little.

When the squash has been in the oven for about 10 minutes, place the quinoa in a saucepan with 250 ml (8½ fl oz/1 cup) cold water. Bring to the boil over a high heat, then reduce the heat to medium, cover and simmer for 15–20 minutes until soft and fluffy. Keep an eye on the quinoa, so it doesn't dry out. Drain and leave to one side.

Roughly chop the herbs and nuts. Then in a large bowl, mix together the quinoa with the cooked squash, herbs, pomegranate seeds, cranberries, nuts and chilli.

Whisk together the dressing ingredients and pour over the salad. Toss to combine, then sprinkle over the orange zest and serve.

# Pork & Quinoa Burgers

**MAKES** 8 (serve 1 or 2 burgers per person)

70 g (2½ oz/ ⅓ cup) mixed red and white quinoa

500 g (1 lb 2 oz) 5% fat minced (ground) pork

3 cm (1 in) piece ginger, grated

3 spring onions (scallions), finely chopped

½ teaspoon smoked paprika

1½ teaspoons harissa

1 tablespoon tamari

juice of ½ lime

freshly ground black pepper

+40 *For the courgette (zucchini) chips*

4 courgettes (zucchinis), cut into wedges

salt and freshly ground black pepper

You won't believe these are so low in calories – they have all the taste but less than half the calories of a regular burger and virtually none of the fat! The quinoa-meat combo also gives you a double whammy of protein, meaning you'll feel totally full and satisfied.

OK, so on non-fast days (or for your non-fasting family) these are great in a bun rather than the lettuce cups, although eating them without the bun does allow you to taste all the flavours more clearly. Mayonnaise is also a good addition and you can sprinkle a tablespoon of Parmesan shavings over when they go in the oven for extra crispness.

The burgers are great to freeze and have ready to go. Once you have shaped them, freeze them on their tray until hard, then pop in a freezer bag. Defrost fully before cooking in the oven as normal.

Place the quinoa in a saucepan with 375 ml (13 fl oz/1½ cups) cold water. Bring to the boil over a high heat, then reduce the heat to medium-low, cover and simmer for 15 minutes until soft and fluffy. Keep an eye on the quinoa, so it doesn't dry out.

Meanwhile, put the pork mince in a large bowl with the ginger, spring onions, smoked paprika, harissa, tamari and lime juice and season with pepper (no salt).

Preheat the oven to 190°C (375°F/Gas mark 5). Line a baking tray with baking paper.

When the quinoa is cooked, drain, run under cold water to cool, and add to the pork.

*Tomato salsa*

4 small tomatoes, chopped

2 spring onions (scallions), chopped

salt and freshly ground black pepper

8 large lettuce leaves

Mix together with your hands. Shape into eight patties using wet hands and place on the prepared tray. Cook in the oven for 40 minutes. Check they are properly cooked all the way through (no pink at all).

When the burgers are in the oven, arrange the courgette wedges on a separate tray. Sprinkle with salt and pepper and cook in the oven for the rest of the burger cooking time – about 35 minutes. They should be cooked through and a little bit brown. They won't be crispy.

Meanwhile, make the salsa by mixing the tomato and spring onions together in a bowl with a little salt and pepper.

Serve the burgers in the lettuce leaves with the chips and salsa.

DINNER

# Snacks & Treats

Snacks and treats can totally derail a fast day, but if you're really struggling, then you do have some options beyond just waiting for the hunger to pass. This chapter has some great lower-calorie ideas to help you through those tough times. Tea and coffee are also good for getting you past the hunger gap – just watch out for those extra calories in any milk you add. Herbal teas or fresh mint tea are probably your best bet – maybe with a slice of lemon to add a bit of extra interest. You can also check out the rye breads, juices, smoothies, muffins and the watermelon crush in the breakfast chapter (see pages 29–53). But if you don't have any calories left at all, then make up a batch of delicious flavoured water (page 149) and keep it in the fridge to sip on – using fizzy water can make these seem a bit more special.

# Coconut Water Ice

**MAKES** 14 cubes

210 ml (7½ fl oz/
¾ cup) coconut
water

*Per cube*

3 redcurrants or
1 small raspberry
or 2 blueberries

These are not meant for mealtimes, but are a great refreshing pick-me-up when you are craving something tasty – but that can't involve crisps. You can, of course, use any fruit you like. Tiny strawberries are great, also chopped fresh apricot or even mango – just avoid anything too big as this makes them harder to eat. I like the tartness of redcurrants here: with the sweetness of the coconut water they really make you feel like you've eaten something far more satisfying than you really have.

Pour the coconut water into the ice cube tray (about 1 tablespoon per cube). Drop in 3 redcurrants, a small raspberry or strawberry or 2 blueberries into each ice cube. You can also mix and match, but don't go crazy. Carefully transport to the freezer and freeze until solid.

# Courgette Fritters

MAKES 12 fritters

2 eggs, beaten

40 g (1½ oz/
⅓ cup) wholemeal
spelt flour

salt and freshly
ground black
pepper

1 teaspoon chilli
flakes

1 courgette
(zucchini), grated

1 teaspoon coconut
or olive oil

squeeze of lemon
juice

Super quick to make and using mostly things you already have in your cupboard, these are best straight from the pan and into your mouth, but they can also be chilled and packed up to eat on the go or for a snack mid-afternoon.

Mix the eggs and flour in a bowl to make a batter. Loosen with 1 tablespoon water. Season with salt and pepper and the chilli flakes.

Mix the courgette into the bowl and stir to coat in the batter.

Heat a non-stick frying pan over a medium heat. Add the coconut oil or olive oil just to grease the bottom of the pan.

Spoon tablespoons of the courgette batter into the pan and cook for 4–5 minutes on each side. They should be lightly browned on both sides and when you break them open, the batter should be cooked all the way through. Repeat with the rest of the oil and the batter. Depending on the size of your pan, you should be able to cook about four at a time.

Serve with a squeeze of lemon juice on top.

If you want to freeze these, leave them to cool, then wrap them up individually in baking paper and freeze in an airtight container. Take them out the night before and leave them in the fridge, then warm through thoroughly in a 180°C (350°F/Gas mark 4) oven for about 10 minutes.

# Popcorn Four Ways

**MAKES** enough for 6 snack-sized portions

60 g (2 oz/¼ cup) popcorn kernels

Shop-bought popcorn has usually been cooked in lots of oil, flavoured with huge amounts of sugar (or salted caramel deliciousness) and topped with extra butter. Not good on a fast day. But the popped corn itself is actually quite a good snack choice. It's pretty high in fibre and also contains lots of health-giving antioxidants. Here is a method for cooking basic plain popcorn (without using any oil) and opposite you'll find some suggestions for toppings that won't blow the diet. This basic recipe comes in at 35 calories per serving.

It will keep for a couple of days in an airtight container, so make a larger batch and portion some off in a snack bag.

Pour the popcorn kernels into a large, heavy saucepan with a lid. They should be in a neat even layer in the bottom – no corn mountains. Cook with the lid on over a medium heat for about 5 minutes. Listen carefully to the kernels popping and shake the pan vigorously every so often. When the popping has slowed down to roughly one every couple of seconds, remove from the heat – better to have a few unpopped kernels than burnt popcorn. Tip into a bowl and leave to cool. You can eat it hot or cold, but if you're packing it up, wait for it to cool completely otherwise it can go a bit soggy.

You can either eat it plain, just with some salt (and pepper) scattered over the top, or add some of your favourite toppings. On fasting days, strong flavours tend to help get us through the hunger gaps.

* plain or salted

## Wasabi Salt

Mix 1 tablespoon wasabi powder with 1 teaspoon salt and scatter over the popped corn.

## Chocolate-Drizzled Popcorn

Melt 40 g (1½ oz/¼ cup) chopped dark chocolate in a microwave or in a small bowl over a pan of simmering water. Don't overheat it. Stir in 1 teaspoon chilli flakes (optional) and drizzle over the popped corn.

## Taste of Italia Popcorn

Mix together 3 tablespoons grated Parmesan with 1 tablespoon Italian herbs (dried from a jar is so much easier, but you can also use chopped fresh herbs if you have the time) and some black pepper. Scatter over the popped corn.

## Cinnamon & Sugar

When only sweet will do, mix 2 tablespoons sugar with 1 tablespoon cinnamon. The cinnamon will help keep your blood sugar levels from rocketing. Scatter over the popped corn.

# Roasted Radishes & Blue Cheese Dip

SERVES 2

80 g (3 oz) radishes (about 10) – mixed colours are pretty, but standard red is fine too

½ tablespoon olive oil

salt and freshly ground black pepper

*For the blue cheese dip*

1 tablespoon low-fat plain yoghurt

15 g (½ oz) blue cheese, like Stilton, crumbled

1 teaspoon apple cider vinegar

Have you ever roasted a radish? They become something totally different – they lose their fire, and taste earthy and sweet. They're best eaten while still warm, but they're also good cold, so make a big batch of these, keep them in the fridge and pop them in a box to take to work. Also, the dip is unbelievable! Cheese! On a fast day?!! Cucumber or celery make a great dipping complement too. The radishes on their own are just under 40 calories per portion if you're running low and can't justify the cheese. Sad times.

Preheat the oven to 200°C (400°F/Gas mark 6).

Toss the radishes in the oil and spread out on a baking tray. Season with salt and pepper. Roast for about 20 minutes, shaking the tray so they cook evenly. They should be soft to the touch but still very firm in the middle.

Meanwhile, make the dip. Combine the ingredients in a bowl with a fork, breaking down the cheese until it's creamy and smooth. If you'd like it a little looser, splash in some water.

# Peanut Butter, Banana & Cherry Milkshake

**MAKES** 2 small glasses

1 tablespoon peanut or almond butter

½ banana, chopped (frozen is better)

5 frozen cherries

250 ml (8½ fl oz/ 1 cup) unsweetened almond milk

OK, so I feel a bit bad about including this as it's really not much of a recipe, but peanut butter is definitely something I turn to when in dire need of a quick fix mid-afternoon. It's full of protein and tastes sweet without actually having any sugar in it. And I couldn't give you a recipe for just eating it with a spoon …

Blitz the banana and cherries in a blender with the almond milk until smooth, then whiz in the nut butter.

# Warming Turmeric & Ginger Nut Milk

**SERVES 1**

250 ml (8½ fl oz/
1 cup) unsweetened
almond milk

½ teaspoon
turmeric

¼ teaspoon ground
cinnamon

¼ teaspoon ground
ginger

½ teaspoon honey

Turmeric milks seem to be everywhere at the moment.
Turmeric has long been believed to have all sorts of healing
and nourishing properties, and its amazing bright colour is
cheering on a slow afternoon. On fast days, high taste for low
calories is what we're after and with this drink, your cup will
be overflowing with flavour!

Gently heat the milk in a small saucepan with the turmeric,
cinnamon and ginger, stirring occasionally. Warm through, but
do not let it bubble.

Pour into your favourite mug, then stir through the honey.

# Serrano Ham
# & Grilled Peaches
## with Thyme

SERVES 2

1 ripe, juicy peach, cut into 8 slices

2 slices of Serrano ham

a few thyme leaves

Cured ham is a taste of holidays. It's salty and delicious and somehow feels like it's too special to be part of a fasting day line up, but go crazy! Combined with grilled peaches, you'll be on a beachfront soaking up the sun somewhere instead of looking at that spreadsheet. If you don't want to grill your peaches, you can chop them up. Just make sure they are juicy and ripe.

Preheat the grill to high. Arrange the peach slices on a foil-lined baking tray. Grill for about 5 minutes, just until they start to colour. Grilling them makes them even sweeter, if you can believe it is possible.

Shred the ham and serve on top of the warm peaches, scattering over the thyme leaves. Alternatively, leave to cool and pack into a box to take with you to work.

# Apple & Cinnamon Crisps

**SERVES 1**

1 medium apple,
cut into thin slices

2 teaspoons
ground cinnamon

These aren't quite the same as a packet of cheese-and-onion, but they will fill that munchy spot mid-afternoon. Take a bag to work to snack on to help you through the post-lunch stretch to the end of the day.

Preheat the oven to 150°C (300°F/Gas mark 2) – don't use the fan setting or your crisps will blow away as they cook.

Toss the apple slices in the cinnamon and arrange on a baking tray.

Cook in the oven for 30 minutes, turning them over halfway through cooking, until they dry out and are slightly browned and a bit crispy at the edges. They won't be quite as crunchy as actual potato crisps, but they will taste totally delicious.

# Banana & Cardamom 'Ice Cream'

SERVES 6

5 ripe medium
bananas (550 g/
1 lb 4 oz total),
sliced and frozen

1 tablespoon
almond butter

½ teaspoon ground
cardamom seeds

It's difficult to believe that this is made from just bananas!
Something magical happens when you freeze bananas –
I think they almost become sweeter and somehow more than
themselves. The basic recipe is just bananas whizzed up, but
I ate banana and cardamon ice cream on holiday once and I
think it makes a nice change – leave it out if you're not keen.
You can also leave out the almond butter, which will reduce
the calories to 85 per serving. Or you can replace it with
2 tablespoons pure cocoa powder (4 calories per serving) for a
chocolatey option, or have it as well as the almond butter for a
luxury version! Play around to find your favourite combination.

Blitz the frozen banana pieces in a food processor until smooth
and creamy. This will take a couple of minutes at least, so do it
in bursts. Don't worry if it seems like it's not doing much to begin
with; it will eventually break down.

When it's looking creamy, add the almond butter and blend,
then scatter over the ground cardamom seeds and blitz again.
That's it!

Pack into a freezable container with a lid and try not to eat it all
at once!

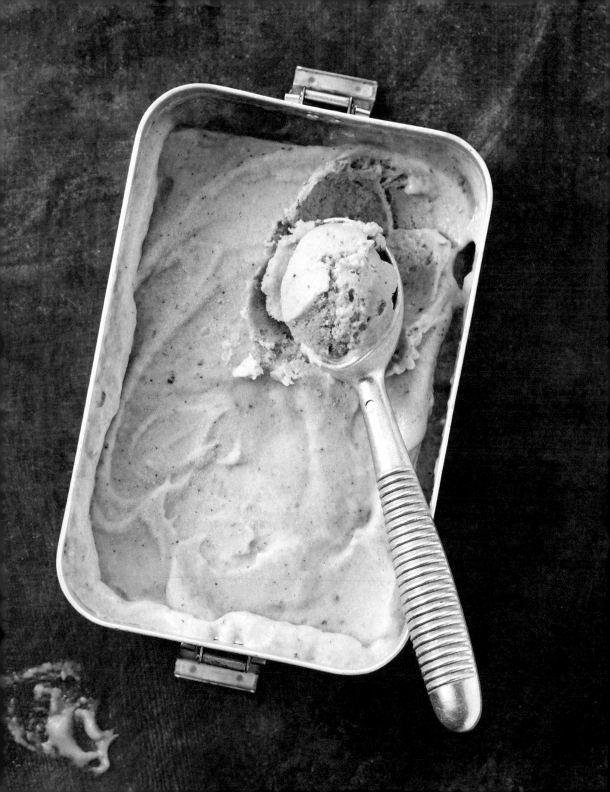

# 100-Calorie Chocolate Chip Cookies

**MAKES 10 cookies**

65 g (2 oz/⅔ cup) oats

35 g (1 oz/⅓ cup) spelt flour

20 g (¾ oz/ ¼ cup) almond flour (ground almonds)

½ teaspoon salt

40 g (1½ oz/scant ¼ cup) demerara (raw) sugar

1 small egg

1 tablespoon maple syrup

2 teaspoons vanilla extract

40 g (1½ oz/ ¼ cup) chocolate chips

I'm all for changing my mindset when following the 5:2. Being more aware of what we are eating, when and what it does to our bodies, are all part of why I think it's such a great lifestyle choice. But sometimes all we need is a cookie. These are full of slow-releasing energy, using spelt, oats and almond flour, meaning you'll get fewer of those sugar spikes.

Preheat the oven to 180°C (350°F/Gas mark 4). Line a baking tray with baking paper.

Combine the oats, flours, salt and sugar in a bowl. In a separate bowl or jug, whisk together the egg, maple syrup and vanilla. Pour the wet ingredients into the dry, along with the chocolate chips, and combine to make a smooth dough.

Spoon little mounds onto the baking tray and squish them down a bit with the back of your spoon. Space them well apart as they spread a bit in the oven. Cook for 10 minutes, then check on them and cook them for another few minutes if they aren't quite ready.

Leave to cool on the tray for a couple of minutes, then transfer to a wire rack to cool completely. Store in an airtight container for up to 1 week.

# Warm Mixed Berries
## with Yoghurt & Pistachios

**SERVES 1**

65 g (2 oz/
¼ cup) goat's
milk yoghurt

40 g (1½ oz/
¼ cup) mixed
berries (e.g.
strawberries,
redcurrants,
blackberries and
raspberries)

4 pistachio nuts,
chopped

When hunger strikes on a fast day, it can be make or break (out the biscuit tin). Since success has a lot to do with preparation, if you haven't anticipated needing a quick-fix, it can often derail all your hard work as you reach for the nearest slice of cake. That's when this recipe comes in – it takes all of 4 minutes to make. No excuses. Quicker than nipping to the corner shop. Of course, you can use different types of yoghurts – just watch the calories.

Gently warm the berries with a splash of water in a small pan over a low heat for 4 minutes or so, until the fruit starts to break down and there's a lovely fruity juice in the bottom of the pan. You don't want the fruit to completely lose its shape though.

Pour the yoghurt into a small serving bowl.

Top with the warm berries and scatter over the nuts.

# Fiery Carrot & Chilli Hummus

MAKES about 16 tablespoons
(2 tablespoons per serving)

150 g (5 oz) carrots, peeled and cut into chunks

½ tablespoon olive oil

salt and freshly ground black pepper

½ × 400 g (14 oz) tin chickpeas (garbanzo beans), rinsed and drained

½ tablespoon tahini

1 teaspoon ground cumin

juice of ½ lemon

2 teaspoons chilli flakes

Hummus is my go-to. That and peanut butter. Whenever I need to fill a hunger (or boredom) gap, hummus comes to the rescue. But even a devout hummus-lover needs to get out on the snack circuit once in a while. Without venturing too far, here are two alternative hummus recipes. They're lovely and colourful, so make dieting more fun.

Dip whatever you like in these. I like to use chicory – it's perfect for scooping, plus I think the bitterness goes well with the creamy hummus. Also radishes, and the usual cucumber and celery. Whatever you like! Obviously keep an eye on the calories.

A good snack portion is 2 tablespoons of hummus plus something green and crunchy – this is about 50 calories.

I'm using half a can of chickpeas in each recipe, but you can double up of course. These will keep, covered, in the fridge for a couple of days.

Preheat the oven to 180°C (350°F/Gas mark 4).

Spread out the carrot chunks on a baking tray and toss in the oil. Season with salt and pepper and cook for 20–30 minutes, until sticky and soft. Remove and leave to cool a little.

Meanwhile, spend a little time peeling off any of the chickpea shells. They can give the hummus a bit of a fibrous texture. Rub them between a clean tea towel and most of them should come off on their own. Don't be obsessive about this though.

When the carrots are cooled, blitz everything together in a food processor or blender. Splash in some water if it needs loosening up. Taste and season with salt and pepper or more cumin.

* 1 tablespoon contains about 20 calories

# Green Herby Hummus

Follow the recipe opposite, but instead of the roasted carrots and chilli, pile in a small handful of freshly chopped coriander (cilantro) and mint leaves and replace the lemon juice with lime juice. Add the same amount of oil as the carrot and chilli hummus but blitz it in with the rest of the ingredients. Grated lime zest on top is also a good addition. This will have slightly fewer calories – around 18 calories per tablespoon.

# No-Calorie Power Water

MAKES 1 litre
(1¾ pints)

OK, so we're clutching at straws here (literally!) but when you're desperate and hungry and you have no calories left to spare, these *may* just help you out of a tight spot and distract you for long enough to forget a rumbling tum and persuade you to hang in there. Maybe. Make a big jug and keep in the fridge for emergencies and make sure it is nice and chilled. Or use sparkling (carbonated) water to make it feel a bit special.

## Cucumber, Ginger & Lemon

Slice 1 cucumber lengthways into strips, using a vegetable peeler. Peel and thinly slice a 5 cm (2 in) piece ginger. Slice an unwaxed lemon. Put them all in a big jug and fill with 1 litre (1¾ pints) water. Chill in the fridge.

## Strawberries & Mint

Thickly slice a handful of strawberries – they're better if they're slightly underripe as they won't turn to mush so quickly. Put them in a big jug with a few sprigs of fresh mint and top up with 1 litre (1¾ pints) water. Chill in the fridge.

## Mint & Fresh Lime

Slice an unwaxed lime and put in a big jug with a few sprigs of fresh mint. Top up with 1 litre (1¾ pints) water and chill.

## Grapefruit & Lemon

Super simple but SO refreshing. Peel a pink or white grapefruit and slice the segments. Put these in a jug with a sliced lemon. Top up with 1 litre (1¾ pints) water and chill.

# Sample Meal Plans

Once you get used to your fasting days you'll discover what works best for you – perhaps you'll prefer to skip breakfast and hold out until lunchtime. Or maybe you'll find you're less hungry if you have just two small snacks during the day and then a bigger evening meal. While you find your way, here are a few meal plans to try.

450 KCAL

## Plan 1

BREAKFAST: Watermelon & Lime Crush
LUNCH: Asparagus with Chopped Egg, Mustard & Capers
DINNER: Spiced Cauliflower Dhal with Fresh Mango Chutney
SNACK: Wasabi Salt Popcorn

## Plan 2

BREAKFAST: Breakfast 'Muffin'
LUNCH: Burrito Bowl
SNACK: Coconut Water Ice
DINNER: Courgette Spaghetti with Creamy Almond Pesto

## Plan 3

BREAKFAST: Flavoured Water
LUNCH: Roast Tomato Bloody Mary Soup
DINNER: Butternut Squash Jewelled Quinoa Salad

## Plan 1

BREAKFAST: Turkish-Style Baked Eggs

LUNCH: Watermelon & Feta Salad

SNACK: Courgette Fritters × 3

DINNER: Sweet Potato & Lentil Curry

SNACK: Coconut Water Ice

## Plan 2

BREAKFAST: Flavoured Water

LUNCH: Wild Rice, Prawn & Mango Salad

DINNER: Cannellini Bean & Chorizo Stew

SNACK: Peanut Butter, Banana & Cherry Milkshake

## Plan 3

BREAKFAST: Rye Slice: Pea & Lemon

LUNCH: Aromatic Chicken Noodle Soup

DINNER: Pork & Quinoa Burger × 1, with Courgette Chips & Tomato Salad

SAMPLE MEAL PLANS

## Plan 1

BREAKFAST: Kale with Bacon
LUNCH: Fig & Goat's Cheese Salad
DINNER: Beef & Lentil Chilli
SNACK: Coconut Water Ice

## Plan 2

BREAKFAST: Quinoa Porridge
SNACK: Serrano Ham & Grilled Peaches
DINNER: Shakshuka
SNACK: Chocolate-Drizzled Popcorn

## Plan 3

SNACK: Warming Turmeric & Ginger Nut Milk
LUNCH: Thai Beef Salad
SNACK: Coconut Water Ice
DINNER: Prawn Summer Rolls × 2 with Dipping Sauce
SNACK: Warm Mixed Berries with Yoghurt & Pistachios

## A Note on Calories

It's important to remember that the exact calorie quantities will differ between brands. The calories in this book have been carefully checked across a range of products, but to be 100 per cent certain, get your scales out and measure out according to the ingredients you use. Unless a large amount of spices and herbs are used in a recipe, these usually haven't been included in the calorie count, as they are such small numbers. And it's also worth noting that these recipes use a 15 ml (½ fl oz) tablespoon.

# Index

INDEX

# Thank You!

A massive thank you to everyone who has helped put this beautiful book together.

To Kajal Mistry at Hardie Grant for being generally just all-round brilliant, to Danielle Wood for the gorgeous photos, and to Ted Allen, Millicent Hawk and Bear the dog for all their assistance. To Nicky Barneby for the fab design, and to Lauren Miller for the lovely props – if only my flat was full of such nice things!

And, most importantly, to Laura Urschel for being a rock during the shoots and a real pal, and who made the food look about as far away from diet food as you can get. THANK YOU!!

Also to my husband, Andy – who ever-so-kindly volunteered to try everything in the book while I was experimenting in the kitchen.

And of course to you, the reader: may your fasting days be full of delicious meals so you never feel 'hangry' again.

# About the Author

Laura Herring is a cookery writer, editor and food consultant. She has worked with many of today's top food writers, bloggers, stylists and chefs around the world, including Sam & Sam Clark, Rachel Khoo, Madhur Jaffrey, Mary Berry, Neil Rankin, and Tom Kerridge.

Laura has written and consulted on a diverse range of cuisines from Nordic to Middle Eastern, French to American, Italian to English, Spanish, American and about subjects as diverse as cakes, pies, pasta, biscuits, barbecue, home-smoking, curing and pickling, curries and... healthy eating.

She currently lives in east London.

ABOUT THE AUTHOR

The Fast Days Cookbook by Laura Herring

First published in 2017 by Hardie Grant Books

Hardie Grant Books (UK)
52–54 Southwark Street
London SE1 1UN
hardiegrant.co.uk

Hardie Grant Books (Australia)
Ground Floor, Building 1
658 Church Street
Melbourne, VIC 3121
hardiegrant.com.au

British Library Cataloguing-in-Publication Data. A catalogue record
for this book is available from the British Library.

ISBN: 978-1-78488-078-1

Publisher: Kate Pollard
Commissioning Editor: Kajal Mistry
Editorial Assistant: Hannah Roberts
Photographer: Danielle Wood
Art Direction: Nicky Barneby
Food Stylist: Laura Urschel
Prop Stylist: Lauren Miller
Copy Editor: Kay Halsey
Proofreader: Laura Nickoll
Indexer: Cathy Heath
Colour Reproduction by p2d

Printed and bound in China by 1010

10 9 8 7 6 5 4 3 2 1